To
Yvonne Williams

Best Work
Coach Stanley

2003

COACH McCRAY

COACH McCRAY:
The Inspiring Story of America's First
Woman Coach of An All-Male Football Team

by

Ms. Shirley Yvonne McCray

in collaboration with
and written by

Dr. Amos Jones, Jr.

BETHLEHEM BOOK PUBLISHERS, INC.
2415 Twelfth Avenue South
Nashville, TN 37204
1997 • BBP

Dedicated to
Jesus, the Head of my life
The late Clara McCray, my grandmother
The late Mable Purnell, my aunt
The late Walter McCray, my father
The late Maratha C. Whitefield, my aunt
Lillian Thompson, my godmother
the thousands of boys and girls
I coached for over 30 years,
and the many coaches and friends
who made this book possible.

∽ CONTENTS ∽

Forward ix

Preface xi

Book I
I.   Coaching One Of My Last Games 1
II.   My Family's Impressions On Me 9
III.   My Passion For The Church 17
IV.   Shaping My Leadership Capabilities 23
V.   How I Was Cultivated To Care For Young
       Black Males. 29

Book II
VI.   TRANSITIONS: My Move From Memphis
       To Chicago 35
VII. Chicago: My Life Touched By Immortals. 43
VIII. The Death Of My Grandmother 49
IX.   My Return To Memphis 57

Book III
X.   Integrating Memphis State University. 61
XI.   Graduating From Memphis State University 71
XII. Introduction To My Career In Teaching. 77

Book IV
XIII. My Coaching Genesis: A Woman Breaking
       Into A Man's World 85
XIV. Coaching With Tears And A Broken Heart 93
XV.   From Chumps To Champs 101
XVI. Flirting With Hollywood 111
XVII. Discrimination, Elimination, Justification 129
XVIII. Lives I Have Touched: The Living Legacy I
       Leave Behind 147

Coach Shirley McCray is one of the finest human beings I have ever known. All I ever needed to know about love, courage, kindness toward others, compassion, self-confidence, self-esteem and belief in myself and my ability, I learned from Coach McCray. She is a tough taskmaster, but she knows how to balance that toughness with charity and support.

Instinctively, I knew when I first encountered Coach McCray at Riverview Jr. High School in Memphis, Tennessee, that our relationship would be special and enduring. My memories of my first encounter with Coach McCray are powerful, touching and quite funny. Try to imagine this powerful, caramel-colored dynamo with a beautiful, lean, healthy, athletic build bellowing out instructions to hundreds of young adolescents in the school hallway during the changing of classes early on a chaotic Monday morning. Other teachers on duty during that same period needed bullhorns or the public address system to be heard or to be recognized or to get the attention of the students — not so for Coach Shirley McCray. We all heard her; knew that we had better obey her and were quite clear that if we did not heed her instructions, we would suffer the consequences. None of us knew what the consequences were and did not want to know. Such was the power and the presence of Coach Shirley McCray in that school.

From afar, I would watch Coach McCray coach girl's volleyball or girl's track. I was drawn to her demeanor and her single-minded dedication, focus and determination to make girls at Riverview excel at sports. I decided that I wanted, indeed, needed, to have someone like Coach to help me to develop the skills and traits that I needed to be successful in life. I decided to begin my relationship with Coach by signing up to be on her track team. I was a gawky thirteen year old with some raw athletic ability, but no focus or discipline. I was smart, but academically unchallenged. Coach McCray changed all of that. She made me work, academically and physically. She helped me to develop discipline and insisted upon dedication and focus in my personal, athletic and academic endeavors.

What began as a relationship between a coach and a young promising athlete became much more than either of us could have ever imagined. For me, Coach McCray became a mentor, a big sister, a surrogate mother, a friend and ultimately, Godmother to my only child,

Franklin Galloway. She is special to me in so many ways that I cannot begin to explore them here. I will summarize by simply saying that Coach McCray embodies all those qualities that God wants Christians to have and she is the finest example that I have seen of the power, the presence and the beauty of the human spirit here on earth. I love her, I adore her and I always will.

Affectionately,
Linda F. Lanton
Student, Friend &
Forever an Admirer
May 5, 1997

∽ PREFACE ∽

This book is being written as a testimony to some of the trials and tribulations endured by me as the first woman to break the barrier of coaching a boy's football team.

It has been my belief that the quality of my work will be reflected by the manner in which the boys and girls I have taught or coached perform as citizens.

My philosophy has been in the words of this song,

"If I can help somebody as I pass along,
If I can cheer somebody with a word or song,
If I can show somebody he/she is going wrong,
Then, my living shall not be in vain."

I do hope the young people touched by me will continue to pass on that touch as they travel through life's Pathway.

I would like to thank all who have supported me in my ups and downs in Coaching and Teaching:

1. Walter McCray, father
2. Clara D. McCray, grandmother
3. Mable D. Purnell, aunt
4. Martha D. Whitfield, Aunt
5. Herman Adams
6. Hosea Alexander
7. Norman Todd
8. Larn Allen
9. Lillian Thompson, godmother
10. Dollie R. Scruggs
11. Hamilton High School Class of '59
12. Principal Elsie Bailey, B.T.W. Faculty, Coaches & Staff
13. Rev. James S. White & the members of the St. Jude Baptist Church
14. Mr. Roosevelt Hodges
15. Lizzie P. Dickerson Alpha Kappa Alpha Sorority (Beta Epsilon Omega)
16. All my many friends and family members not mentioned who prayed for me

And most of all the young men and women I've coached at:

Riverview Jr. High
Chickasaw Jr. High
Kingsury High School

Geeter Jr. High
Booker T. Washington
Lanier Jr. High

xi

BOOK I

CHAPTER I

COACHING ONE OF MY LAST GAMES

When the One Great Scorer comes
to write against your name —
He marks — Not that you won or lost
— but how you played the game.

Grantland Rice

The 4th day of January 1995 was one of those cold, damp winter days in Memphis. My day had started as it had for almost twenty-eight years, responding to that rigorous routine of rising early and maneuvering out into the rush and rumble of Memphis traffic to get to school. The circuit of my public school teaching career had brought me to the celebrated Booker T. Washington High School. I had taught successfully at any number of junior high schools and now I had been placed at prestigious Booker T. Washington High School to do what I had learned and loved to do, coach boys in football and basketball. In my early years, I had coached track, volleyball, tennis, and any number of other sports. I had coached girls in my lifetime. But over the course of years, I gained a passion for coaching young men. I guess there was a strong reason for this direction in my life.

I had not slept well the night before, it was something that had grown on me as the passion for coaching captivated me early in life. Quite often, my desire to win, or at least put on a good showing, had driven me with such force, excited me so that my adrenaline lurched and raced to a pitch of fever. I just couldn't sleep most nights before I had a game. I constantly went over the plays, one by one, play by play, to be sure of each player's execution and to determine what player would perform the best. So had it been the night before.

When I arrived at school that morning, I routinely went through my classroom presentations; but in all sincerity, my mind was on the game I had at Melrose that afternoon. My boys were in my class in physical science. I was both their teacher and coach. I tried to instill in the players a sense of the need to learn and to become somebody through what they knew as well as what they did on the football field or basketball court. So, with one eye on the game that afternoon and one eye on the lesson presentations, I went through the routine of

1

the day, I proceeded to teach and inspire in the classroom as I had sought to do for many years on the football field and basketball court.

In teaching my class in health and physical education, quite often I found myself dealing with the subject matter in terms of dress codes and hygiene. I had a penchant for having the boys wear shirts and ties to school. My philosophy was that basketball and football players should be leaders, which meant that they dressed the part, among other things. I have to admit, though, as I taught my class that day, my mind was on that game.

As school was being dismissed for the day, I began to gather up the players on my Junior Varsity basketball team in preparation for the game. I was "Coach McCray," and a very successful "Coach McCray!" I had had championship teams and outstanding players. I was privileged to be cited as the nation's first and only female coach of an all male football team. I had received many accolades, prizes and awards. But, here I was, "Coach McCray," for the love of the game and my burning desire to help young Black boys become something, serving not only as coach but as trainer, equipment manager, and team physician as well. I had worked hard to make certain the boys were in good physical shape. I made sure they exercised and drilled so their physical condition was not lacking. I also made sure they did not have ailments I did not know about, which could hamper them or even worse keep them from playing that afternoon.

Once I made certain all things were ready at the school, I bothered myself with the perfunctory chore of picking up the boys to carry them to the game site. I took my van and packed the players like sardines off to Melrose. Anthony Phillips was real tall, but I crammed him into the van. Jimmy True was a good bit smaller so I squeezed him beside Anthony Phillips and another player who was a great deal larger than little Jimmy. But, the little fellow sat right on in there and rode like a champ.   We were pinned up against one another. Really, the truth of the matter was that these boys would never get to the game were it not for me providing transportation for them. After all these years, I found that coaching involved all these things, from the rugged to the ridiculous; from the daring to the distasteful; and from the unthought of to the unthinkable. Yes, there were even times I had to be even the daddy and the mamma.

We finally arrived at Melrose for the game. I summoned the boys into the locker room where and I told them to get dressed and afterward I wanted to talk with them. Once dressed, I called them together and began to give my pep rally. I said to them, as I had said so many times, "Do as I have taught you." I felt I had taught them every-

2

thing they needed to know to be successful on the floor that afternoon. As important as playing basketball, I had taught them self assurance and pride in themselves. Many of my players over they years had been babies of mothers addicted to crack cocaine. Some of these young men fitted into that category. In so many cases, the boys had serious psychological problems and sometimes uncontrollable behavioral problems. Low self esteem, defaced self image, lack of self assurance all played themselves out in the lives of these young boys. So I continued to drill into them the basics of life. I had even taken them to church in order to instill in them the power of prayer and security in Jesus Christ. Most of these young boys had not even seen the inside of a church nor did they know the advantages and strengths of the Christian Faith and being a member of the church. I had tried to make this available to them.

So, that afternoon I challenged them: "I have taught you how to play this game, now it is up to you to play it." The soldierly, driving instinct I learned from my father came into play as I barked out instructions to them: "Defense, cover your man. On offense, make your shots count." I made assignments to each player, defensive as well as offensive. I did not have the best feeling about winning this game. There just was not the feeling I got when I was virtually assured of a win. Nevertheless, after all of the pre-game particulars, I called the boys together for prayer. We never thought to enter a game without team prayer. I had gotten the boys so accustomed to the prayer entry in our schedule that they would never let me forget to led them in prayer. They would remind me if it seemed I was going to forget to lead them in prayer. As we concluded our prayer, I charged them to go out and win one for me. They took off running onto the gym floor with as much enthusiasm as I have ever seen any of my teams. Even with their deficiencies, I was happy to see them give me the assurance they would do the best they could.

With a pensive eye, as was always the case, I watched my boys go through their warm-up exercise. They looked pretty good. They were making their layups and set shots. But, I still had some reservation about their ability to beat this team from Melrose.

My boys finished their warmup and prepared for the tipoff. I called them to the sidelines where I gave them some last minute instructions and led them in a pep talk and prayer. I had given the lineup in the locker room. The young men took the floor and they were ready for the tipoff.

The tipoff by the center of Booker T. Washington did not fare so well that afternoon. In the early moments of the game, the team galloped up and down the court, never able to keep up with what already had become obvious, a superior Melrose team. I sat rather tensely watching the team race up and down the floor. My boys could not keep up with their torrid pace. We never gained the lead. We came as close as two points but fell back four and sometimes six.

Things got so that I could not hold my peace. My boys fought back gallantly but consistently lost grip and fell farther and farther behind. I leaped to my feet. At first, I said nothing; I just wanted to let the boys know I was not pleased with the results of their play. I then began to blast trumpet-like commands in an attempt to take control of the game. It was as though I were at the ringside, getting ready to go against my opponent. The more I watched my boys run up and down the floor with no measurable results, the more I became animated and vocal. My voice pierced the gymnasium air with verbal commands. It ricocheted against the half filled bleachers and the cavernous gymnasium, barking orders and directions.

The merciful relief of half time came not too soon. I was relieved when the buzzer sounded announcing the end of the first half. I followed my boys into the locker room with many things on my mine. I had not conceded the loss to Melrose; however, I increasingly felt we did not have a good chance. I turned my mind to what I could say to enhance the intellectual, moral, ethical, and spiritual state of the players. How can I lead these young men to become "thinking individuals?" What could I do to share with them the kinds of things I had learned in the church? I decided that would be the thrust of my half time talk.

The boys took care of their bodily needs, got water and went to the rest room. They sort of stood around momentarily collecting themselves from the razzle and dazzle of the first half. Then, I called them to huddle in front of me as I stood before the chalkboard. I began my talk, which I hoped would prepare them for the second half. "I have taught you how to play this game, but you will have to play it." I began with a passion that I hoped would reach both their head and heart. I continued, "I want a sound team. When you start doing what I tell you to do, we will win a game." I plaintively appealed to them to employ obedience and respect for authority. I found myself verbalizing my distress, in a sense, in my disapproval of them not measuring up to my high standard. I chastised them, "You are the same ones who will not wear shirts and ties like I tell you."

But then, after I finished my verbal flagellation, I turned to the second half of the game. I became upbeat in my talk. "What is your number?" I asked each of the young men who was to start the second half. I charged them and verbally drove them, "I want pressure, pressure, pressure!" "I want pressure on defense." The boys leaped to their feet to rush out of the locker room. Their eyes were burning with the fires of determination. They did not want to let me down. They wanted to win this game for Coach McCray!

My boys were a different team from the first half. They fought Melrose point for point. I was overcome with emotion. I shouted from the sidelines both instructions and encouragement. "Good comeback," I shout encouragement to them as they scored a point and rushed back down the floor to position themselves on defense. As they got back on defense, I continued to instruct and encourage them: "Good comeback!" "Now, don't foul and don't let them make no threes."

My boys played their hearts out. But try as they may, they could not pull out the game for me. Sporadically, my boys played a bit sloppily and I called them to the sidelines and said to them, "Hey, think!" while I pointed to my head to get my point over. But the Melrose boys simply outplayed us and outscored us.

When the buzzer sounded the end of the game, the scoreboard blazed the score — Melrose 46-Booker T. Washington 43. My boys came off the floor exhausted, with beads of perspiration cascading down their face and beading all over their body. At first, none of the boys came to the huddle as they were taught. They wandered about in somewhat of a daze. Some of them leaned up against the bleachers which had not been let out as seats, because not too many people were expected. They looked into space, panting and allowing the adrenaline to bleed off and their bodies to stabilize.

I took this opportunity to inspect the injuries of some of my boys. One of the boys limped about aimlessly up and down the sidelines. He grimaced in pain. Anguish from physical discomfort was written large across his face. "Sit down, let me see that ankle," I said. I stooped down and flexed his ankle to his acquiescing displeasure. "You think you need to go to the hospital?" I said, looking up into his youthful face contorted with pain and anguish. I suppose his pride prevented him from agreeing to medical attention. "No coach, I think I'll be alright."

The other young man was not so fortunate. He was one of my forwards and had taken an elbow to the chin. I feared he may have suffered dislodged teeth while battling under the boards for a loose ball. "You need to go to the hospital!" I said with sympathetic authority. After awhile, the young man conceded to my insistence that he be hospital bound, as he looked up from the sideline bench with a damp towel to his bleeding mouth.

I called them all together and had some parting words for them. "We

Coach McCray admires one of her championship football teams.

are going to have to do better! Is that right gentlemen?" In unison, they responded almost glumly, "Yes ma'am!" But that was as far as I wanted to go with that tone of speech. I did not want to fray their feelings any further or plunge them further into the pit of despair. I dare not disparage them for not winning. I wanted them to win, but I wanted them to learn some more important lessons than winning a basketball game — maybe at any cost. That was not the way I wanted them to play the game. I simply wanted them to know that they had played a good game but had not measured up to what I had taught. Satisfied that I had gotten that message over, I sought to share with them the soothing oil of compassion and the comforting pillow of sympathy.

After calming them down and assuring them that they had given a representative showing, I called them to prayer. They all rushed to encircle me, slapping their hands on top of mine and each other's thereafter. We all began to pray:

> *Our Father, which art in heaven,*
> *Hallowed be Thy Name,*
> *Thy kingdom come,*
> *Thy will be done,*
> *On earth as it is in heaven.*
> *Give us this day our daily bread,*
> *And forgive us our debts*
> *As we forgive our debtors;*
> *And lead us not into temptation,*
> *But deliver us from evil.*
> *For thine is the kingdom,*
> *And the power,*
> *And the glory,*
> *Forever. Amen!*

After the prayer, the boys broke reverently from the prayer huddle to make their way back home. The ones I brought loaded up in my van. I took the healthy ones home first. Afterwards, I took the injured to the hospital. This was a very familiar ritual for me, for I had spent my life being mother and father, doctor and lawyer, disciplinarian and policewoman; in fact, I had been everything for my players, including Coach McCray. We had not won the game, but I had been for my boys what they needed to become somebody in life. Hopefully, for some young boy on that team something will come of him, that he will grow up to become somebody. My dad, grandmother, and aunt had worked hard for me to become somebody, I wanted to pass this blessing on to somebody else.

On the sidelines of one of her last basketball games.

Halftime instruction

CHAPTER II

MY FAMILY'S IMPRESSIONS ON ME

> The more intensively the family has stamped its character upon the child, the more it will tend to feel and see its earlier miniature world again in the bigger world of adult life.
>
> Carl Jung

My family left on me impressions which have lasted to this day. My church, father, grandmother, and aunt's signature are indelibly imprinted on my psyche, soul, my life and my very being. It is without a doubt that what I have become, the accomplishments I achieved during my lifetime, I owe to my family, these three great and strong personalities.

On November 17, 1941, I was born in Cook County Hospital, Chicago, Illinois. My father, Walter McCray, was a military man. Of my mother, I know not much. My father had been in the military but had gotten out for a brief period. It was during the brief time he met my mother that I was conceived. That was in February of 1941. I was born in November of 1941. But, the yearn for the life of discipline which the military provided would not give relief to my father. He was tormented with this desire. He was a hard working man, a man driven by passion for work, work, and more work. In his own way, he was a perfectionist at whatever he did. Not finding refuge from the ever menacing desire to re-enter the military, my dad decided to leave again for the Army. Just before entering the military the second time during the war, my mother became pregnant again. She gave birth to a son, my younger brother, Nathaniel, the only other sibling I had in the world. In the course of time, my father and mother moved back to Chicago from Memphis.

When my father left for the military, it was not long before my mother, Dorothy, took me to my father's mother, Clara McCray in Memphis. At six months of age, while I

My father, Walter McCray

Grandmother Clara Dean McCray and Shirley, an inseparable combination.

of age, while I was in diapers, my mother took me to Memphis. For a long time, all this lay in the thick shroud of mystery. I do know I never heard from my mother again. I later learned that she died at age 27 from a cerebral hemorrhage. Although my mother fades into the obscure fabric of yesterday, my father's impression is etched in my very character and can never be erased.

I cannot remember much about my early days in Memphis. My grandmother told me of them. In reality, those were the days which gave shape to my life till now. I was in diapers when my grandmother, Clara McCray, took me in. Mamma, as I knew her, raised me in my early years, until my father returned from the military. She was exactly what I needed. She was loving, honest and kind. However, Mamma could be very strict and very protective of me. There was nothing she would not do for me, often doing without so I might have what I needed. Over the years, we grew very close, to the point of being inseparable. Whenever you saw Clara McCray, you saw her grand daughter Shirley.

My grandmother was tough. She was rugged, able to endure immeasurable burden and pain. My grandmother had to live a great deal of her life without a husband. It is believed that grandfather died of yellow fever, however, it was some years after the yellow fever epidemic of 1878 ended. My grandmother did not succumb to life without a husband, she became the matriarch of the home place at Cummings and South Parkway. Without any help, she raised her own five children. They consisted of the twins Hazel and William, Samuel, Robert, and my father Walter. She also helped raise her sister's ten children. When my mother brought me back to Memphis, my grandmother never wavered or wondered what to do. She simply took on the responsibility of raising her son's child. Now that I look back on her decision, I am so glad she did. I do not know what kind of person I would be had any other kind of decision been made.

My grandmother was very religious. She knew her Bible very well. She believed in the Word of God. She was a true born Christian and a thoroughbred Baptist. She was one of the organizers of our home church, St. Jude Baptist Church on Emerson Street in Memphis. Since 1898, she had been a member of that church. She was never a member of another church. St. Jude was her church until she died. She was a trustee of the church. She loved her church so much that she was there all the time. For one reason or other, she was at church every night of the week and on Saturdays and Sundays as well. In fact, she held practically every position in the church which could be held. She was church treasurer. She was president of the Mother's Board. She was Sunday school teacher for Class No. 10, which was an all male class of younger boys and men. She was the "money raising" person in our church. She had a personality which made people want to cooperate with her. So, when she set out to raise money, she was always successful because people wanted to help her. She was a born leader who knew how to get people to follow her. Then, on Saturdays, my grandmother never failed to go to the church to clean up the building. When I got old enough, I always helped her. It happened that no matter what was going on at the church, if my grandmother went, I was there with her. Wherever she was, there I would be also. Her church routine became a fixture in my mind, to the point that to this day I can yet remember what happened each night:

Monday - 12 Noon	Missionary Meeting
Tuesday night	Usher Board Meeting
Wednesday night	Prayer Meeting
	Choir rehearsal
Thursday night	Sunshine Band - Young Adult
Friday night	Red Circles - Teen Group
Saturday	Church clean up day
Sunday - all day	Church
9:15 a.m.	Sunday school
11:00 a.m.	Worship service
5:00 p.m.	Baptist Training Union
7:00 p.m.	Sunday night service.

This routine became so seated in my mind that I knew it backwards. We were at the church almost every time the doors opened. I went whether I wanted to or not. Church came to be a real part of my life, a part of which in fact I did not regret then nor do I regret now.

My grandmother often talked to me of how I was the baby in the church. She carried me in my diapers and pretty little dress, with all of the little frills and bows. I became everybody's darling. Because I was the only baby in the church, everybody raised me. Everybody spanked me as well.

A friend of my grandmother, Ada Robertson, once told me of one occasion while in diapers I went to the pulpit and got into Pastor Mosby's spittoon. She told me that my grandmother did not like that so well, and tapped me on my bottom — according to her report. I always liked to hear the preacher preach at church. I suppose I had not approached my first birthday when I took advantage of Mamma's patent position of having her eyes closed during the sermon. Pastor Mosby was preaching that Sunday morning. He was deep into his sermon. Baptist preachers in the Negro Baptist Church had a way with preaching. They can tell the Bible story till saints all over the church house get the Spirit and become emotionally swept away into spiritual euphoria.

Pastor Mosby had a rhythm he would get while preaching. With it, he rocked the church. On top of that, he had a musical voice which sang out his sermon. By the time he got to his conclusion, he would let out a melodic exclamation which was not a shout, scream, squeal, or sqwack. What Pastor Mosby did amounted to the development of a well-tuned and carefully toned intonation at the conclusion of his sermon. Once he did that, after he had well-told the Bible story, something divinely terrible happened. Ushers held Sis. Thomas so she would not hurt anybody when she flung her arms in the air. Jimmy Justintime, our pianist, slid off the piano bench and onto the floor screaming in the spirit. Sis. Marina Solomon threw her pocketbook through the air and Sis. Clarresa Slaughter flung her handkerchief straight up above her head.

While this was happening, Sis. Robertson told me later in life that as Pastor Mosby was preaching and eyes were reverently closed, I quietly slipped away from her and proceeded to the pulpit. He chewed tobacco and would always go to the pulpit with a wad of the juice producing stuff in his mouth. It seems he could never really preach unless he had a cut of juicy tobacco in his mouth. While preaching, he spat in a spittoon he had conveniently placed beside the pulpit. Once he had spat, he collected himself and went back to preaching. While he was preaching, I crawled up on the pulpit rostrum and began to play with the spittoon. Pastor Mosby never noticed me while he was preaching. One of the members saw me and came and grabbed me up from under the pastor's feet. Some of the members were humored by what I did; I have been told that while I was a baby, I became the church clown. My grandmother gave me a little spanking for that. I never lost my love for preaching about Jesus or the church.

My grandmother taught me to love the church. We were there 365 days a year. I guess there was not much else for me to do, learn, or love to do. She was not only serious in her religious practice, but in her dress as well. On Sunday she always wore a white dress. She was a mother of the church. She never wore flashy clothes in any respect. Her shoes were black with shoestrings and medium heels. She wore bland cotton stockings with strings which held them up.

Mamma's children had to behave. All of us were trained to behave. When she'd sit in her white dress in the Mother's Board corner, it always seemed that her eyes were closed. But, they were not closed so much that she did not know and hear everything that went on in the church. She had a saying, "Everyone with their eyes closed are not always sleep." That was ever so true! When she opened her eyes and looked at you, she had a way of doing so that made you change your attitude. The way she talked to you, if she had to say something to you, your attitude would change real fast. Mamma was a real disciplinarian.

Grandmother could cook. She was known for her "T" Cakes. She baked them all the time. Most of the time, however, her "T" Cakes were baked for the church, to raise money for the church. There was hardly any time when she did anything for herself, it was all done for the church or someone else. She was always doing something for others. She took in washing and ironing from white folk in order to earn money enough for the two of us. She sold "T" cakes in order to raise money to give to her boys in the Sunday school class, to have something to put in their collection. Quite often she would neglect herself for others.

During my early years, my grandmother taught me so much. She taught things my little mind could grasp, but she'd say them in such a way and so often that I never forget what she said. She taught me to love God and live for him. I think by taking me to church 365 days a year conditioned me to live the godly life and love God with all my heart. One thing she constantly said to me took root in my little soul and never lost its grasp. She said, "Finish school, be somebody, love God always, put Him first and your blessings will be added to you." I found out later, those words would guide me through life. I never forgot those words. With the fire and fervor of faith, she burned them into my very being, my mind, soul, and spirit.

When my father returned from the military, he took up residence in

Chicago, where I was born. The family established a practice of letting me stay in Memphis during the main course of the year and spend summers in Chicago. This went on for some time, until I completed high school.

This exchange provided opportunity for my dad to fix his imprint on my life. What a job he did of that! As I look back on that time in my life, his characteristic of a loving and kind spirit was irradically imprinted in me. My dad was a work-a-holic. He worked three jobs sometimes — with hours ranging from 3:00 a.m. in the morning till 7:00 p.m. at night. He worked hard so I could have the basics. Regardless of the times or circumstances, he always saw to it that I had clothes like dresses, skirt, blouse, dress shoes and school shoes, black and white oxfords.

My dad's generosity toward me did not prevent him from being very strict. He was stern! In fact, it was my dad who gave me my first "real" whipping. It was about a little boy. I called myself taking up a relationship with a boy without my father's approval. I paid for that with a severe price. I will never forget that experience.

My dad taught me the importance of work. He taught me how to work. When I was old enough, he taught me how to wash windows, mop floors, clean toilets, cut yards, do minor plumbing, electrical work, and even car repair. He taught me to do it the correct way. His reasoning for teaching me those things was that if I did them then, maybe I would not want to do them the rest of my life and would seek some different and higher goals. His hope was that such experiences would lead me to go on to college, finish college, be somebody, do what he did not do. Before he died, his dreams and desires came to fruition in my life.

One last dynamic and truly great force in my life was Aunt Mable Dean Purnell. She was sister to my grandmother. The two of them were very close. They had very similar characteristics. Aunt Mable was loving, kind, and honest. Her strictness received the respect she expected. She had a way with words, like Mamma. Also like Mamma, she had a look which got across the message she wanted and drew out the results

Aunt Mable Dean Purnell

she expected.

Like my grandmother, Aunt Mable was very religious and extremely community minded. She went to church at St. Jude as often as my grandmother. She was as involved in the church as well. She organized a Sunday school class for "back-sliders." That was a class for church members who had started to attend but had fallen by the way-side. She had a habit of calling these persons on Saturday and early Sunday morning to remind them to come to Sunday school. She was quite successful! Most of the people she called and harassed came to Sunday school. She was president and treasurer of women's clubs both in and out of the church. A great singer, she sang in many choirs, St. Jude Baptist Church Choir, the Western Regional Choir of the Tennessee Baptist Missionary and Educational Convention, and the Southern Christian Women's Choir to name a few. She was like her sister in so many ways. Another of which was her ability to raise money for the church. Aunt Mable was a great cook. Nobody could beat her "chittlin' dinners." People kept coming for more, because they knew she could cook chittlins'. All the money she made went to the church, just like my grandmother.

Aunt Mable had a way of communicating with people. She was dignified. She carried herself in a high fashion. Her dress was immaculate and elegant. She was a pretty woman. Because of her dress decor and personal demeanor, she got along great with people. She was a people person. It is little wonder that almost all of her life, for 25 years, she successfully sold insurance for North Carolina Mutual Life Insurance Company. Aside from this, she and her husband, Uncle Thomas, raised 13 children.

I am indebted to Aunt Mable for many things. For one, she, like my grandmother encouraged me to make something of myself. She consistently said to me, "Do your best so you can be somebody and make something of yourself." She was the major influence in my life to go on to college. In fact, she spent her own money so I could go to college and complete school at Memphis State University.

These were the major mortal forces which impacted my life as a young girl growing up in Memphis, Tennessee and the southside of Chicago. Like the hands of skilled artists, my church, my father, my grandmother, and my aunt sculpted my mind, body, and spirit. They introduced me to God who gave me the spiritual power to be propelled to the zenith of history in the field I would later come to love, sports. They introduced me to the church which was the community of fellowship which welcomed me and ministered to me and accepted me, and made me feel wanted and loved. Finally, they introduced me to the disciplines of life, without which I would have been beaten by the vissicitudes of life and dashed against jagged boulders of destruction by boisterous winds of life which blew without favor. Without my family, I could never become whatever God made me to be.

CHAPTER III

MY PASSION FOR THE CHURCH

Remember now thy creator in the days of thy youth, while the evil days come not, nor the years draw nigh, when thou shalt say, I have no pleasure in them.

Ecclesiastes 12:1

Family life was a real blessing for me in my early life. My grandmother provided a warm and close atmosphere in our home at Cummings and South Parkway. Although there were many family members living at the home place, we did not know inconvenience. Each family member supported the other.

Mamma, as I came to know my grandmother, was the bedrock, the anchor, the cornerstone of the whole family. Without a husband — granddaddy had died in the early 1900's from the Yellow Fever Epidemic which ravaged Memphis since 1878 — and without any help, Mamma raise us all and never left the house. She took in washing and ironing from white folk and made her money that way. There was no welfare in those days, but we never wanted for anything.

My church became the extended family for me, just as the home place was at Cummings and South Parkway. My grandmother was an anchor in St. Jude Baptist Church on Emerson Street, just like she was at home. She was one of the congregation's founding members. When I was old enough to remember, I can recall her taking me to church. She would be dressed in her white uniform, just like she was every Sunday — all day. She sat as a saint in the mother's board corner, reverently meditating with eyes closed. Every time you saw her in church, that was the way she was. When she prayed, she was especially sincere and spiritually moving. There was something in my little soul, even as a child, that I could feel when grandmother prayed. There was a strange kind of assurance and inner satisfaction that came over me whenever she prayed. She exuded something of a staying power to the soul when you looked at her in such a solid, secure, saintly, and stately demeanor.

Mamma's emotional state changed when the spirit began to move in the church. *SHINE ON ME* was her favorite song. Whenever she'd sing it, tears flowed down both her cheeks and tied neat knots underneath her chin. Many are the days I remember looking up at her smooth unadorned face and seeing those tears as she sang her favorite song. Then, when Reverend Mosby got to preaching, spiritual animation seized her. There was no jumping and shouting as such, just a subdued and often almost inaudible "preach it," could be heard. Her witness most often was muffled by the loud shouts and affirmations which flooded that little church by the hungry souls which rushed to that spiritual table each Sunday. Her faith in God was so deep that it never seemed necessary for her to make much noise about her trust in Him for her life. But when Reverend Mosby started preaching, she had a little rhythmic rock from side to side that slowly consumed her and seemed to gently carry her into some other kind of world that was totally spiritual.

As early as I can remember, my grandmother took me to Sunday school. She told me later in life that I was in Sunday school even in the Cradle Roll Class, then in Kindergarten and Primary and so on. It was about my fourth year in the world when I began to know what was going on in life. It was about then that I remember my days in Sunday school. I learned about Jesus and His love. It must have been when I was about two or three years old when I remember coloring Jesus and his disciples. The Sunday school material had little cutouts that I liked, they seemed to put me right into the Bible story. Mamma had talked to me constantly about Jesus. She told me that He loved me and she taught me the little song:

> *Jesus loves me, this I know*
> *For the Bible tells me so,*
> *Little ones to Him belong,*
> *They are weak but He is strong.*
>
> *Yes, Jesus loves me,*
> *Yes, Jesus loves me,*
> *Yes, Jesus loves me,*
> *For the Bible tells me so.*

Because of my exposure to The Bible at home, I came to love Sunday school. When we sang *"Jesus Loves Me,"* because Mamma had taught it to me, I would just throw my little head back and sing aloud with conviction. In fact, I came to love the church. I knew nothing else. I did not want to know anything else!

My aunt Mable was a part of the church family at St. Jude. She sang in the choir. She liked to sing Dr. Brewster's songs. *"How I Got Over"* and *"Move On Up A Little Higher"* were some of the songs she loved. She had a habit of waving her hand as she sang, pitching her head from side to side, as if to kind of show off her freshly pressed and curled hair. Now Aunt Mable would shout! Mamma hardly ever shouted, but Aunt Mable? She would get loose every now and then.

But not only was Mamma and Aunt Mable in the church, my whole family was in the church. This did something **for** me and **to** me. In the first few years of my life, I came to know nothing but family and church. In the friendly, familiar, and fortifying confines of home and church, I was nurtured, instructed, spiritually led and fed, and encouraged. In this context, my grandmother seemed never to cease to say to me, "Shirley, grow up to be somebody, love God always, put Him first and your blessings will be added to you." Over time, that saying became etched on the tablet of my psyche and my soul.

The fellowship of the church was fascinating to me. Even at four and five years of age, I remember the great times we had in church activities. Mamma took me to picnics. I remember them well. We went to Lincoln Park in South Memphis. The youth played each other in baseball games. Sometimes when their real ball gave out, unraveled or just disintegrated, they played with the core which was made of rags. They played with that until it unraveled so much that they could not play any more. When the ball game was over, the kids played sack races. Some of the young boys played marbles for their recreation. While they did all that, I frolicked about like a little butterfly, carefree and having fun. I could never forget all the food we had. Especially good were the French Fries. Of course, Mamma did not miss the opportunity to sell dinners in order to raise some money for the church and her Sunday school class.

Like home, church was a real part of my life, almost from the very first day I was born into the world. My grandmother took me to church everyday. When I was big enough, I helped her clean up the church building on Saturdays so we could be ready for church on Sundays. She carried me to all the meetings of the church, usher board meetings, choir rehearsals, trustee board meetings, business meetings, and so on. Whatever was going on at the church, my grandmother had business there; and, she carried me. Sundays, all day, were devoted to singing and praying and studying the Word of God at church.

So, church was a real part of the formative years of my life. And, the more I was taken to church, the more I was in church, the more I wanted church to be in me. As I was approaching 8 years old, the urge to join church began to crowd in on me irresistibly. I was only 8 years old, but I knew exactly what was happening to me. I wanted to be in the church. Whatever this was that made Mamma the person she was and whatever it was that made Aunt Mable the kind of person she was, I wanted the same thing. As far as I could see, the home and church were the forces which gave shape to their lives. I wanted the same thing to happen to me.

An extraordinary feeling that can be liken to nothing but a spiritual surge came over me to join the church. It was something irresistible. Eight years old, but there it was, this spiritually moving feeling I could not explain. All I knew was that I wanted to be in the church. Everybody was doing something in the church, it seemed, except me. All the big kids were involved in something in the church; but as the littlest one in the church, I was always left out. I wanted to be involved in church life like everyone else. I had been influenced by what I had seen of my grandmother and all the other members of my family and I also had been affected by the older youth in the church. I wanted to be like them, to get involved in the church. The only way I figured this could happen was to join the church.

I had asked earlier in my life if I could join the church. Mamma would not allow me at the time. I was too young, she said. But I kept asking. I just wanted her to know I wanted to be a Christian, I wanted to be in the church. I had been taught about Jesus, about what it meant to be a Christian. Church had been a part of my life, all my life. So, I wondered why I had to wait so long before I joined.

Now as I look back, I realize what was happening. During those times, they just did not allow anyone to join the church simply because they wanted to. The preacher, deacons, and leaders of the church had to be sure you had something. They sometimes referred to it is "having religion." You had to "get this religion" before they accepted you in the church. It had to be heart-felt, spirit-born, and life-changing. You really had to be born again. Although I was only eight years old, I thought I had all that.

I had gone to the mourner's bench about two or three times before they let me join the church. Now, the mourner's bench was up at the front of the church. That was the front pew where unbelievers sat when the revival was in session. The church mourned over them till they came through. Sometimes parents and grandparents gathered around the unbelievers and prayed over them until they confessed Jesus Christ as their Savior. Sometimes, which was not very often, there would be someone who the church prayed over and they still would not join the church. But most of the time, the prayers of the saints brought fourth a new born child of God. When that happened, there would be joy in the church. The saints of the church shouted that another child of God had been born. Those were some moving experiences.

I remember when little Sammy Junior joined the church. We had a week's revival and Reverend Mosby was preaching. Little Sammy Junior sat on the mourner's bench all week. On Thursday night, his grandmother went up there and sat beside him. She just sat there with her head sort of bowed as she listened to Reverend Mosby's sermon. It was a moving sermon, people witnessed and even shouted in response to his preaching of The Word of God. When Reverend Mosby opened the doors of the church for anyone to come forth to become a member of the church, Sammy Junior's grandmother got up and stood by her grandson. Little Sammy Junior had been sort of a tough youngster, he had kind of gone for bad. But, he sat there that night looking straight ahead as though he was unmoved by what was going on. Reverend Mosby appealed to him with strong and moving words which were delivered right from the fiery furnace of his soul. When he did not get up and go forward to Reverend Mosby, his grandmother knelt down beside him and started to pray. She prayed one of the most heartfelt prayers you ever wanted to hear. She prayed in a musical fashion, which is so familiar in the Negro Baptist Church. She was almost crying, there was a weep in her voice, a plaintive lament. But her prayer was directed straight at Sammy Junior as much as it was directed to God. She wanted him to ". . .give his life to The Lord," she prayed. "Lord, help my grandson to come out of the world." Her plaintive cry rose in crescendo-like fashion, with a sort of feeble tremble that pierced the heart and penetrated the soul. I could not see how Sammy Junior could sit there. I wanted to get up for him. "Lord!" she cried, "Save my son. Turn him around while he's on turning ground." Tears streamed down her face and she wiped them daintily with her handkerchief in between heartrending sobs and supplications.

Well, I guess little Sammy Junior could not withstand the spiritual power his grandmother's prayers had with The Lord. Something overcame him so much so that he abandoned his state of coolness that he was known for in the neighborhood and broke down in tears like his grandmother. He stood up from his seat on the front pew and stepped forward and gave his hand to Reverend Mosby who was standing nearby. Sammy Junior's conversion made me want the day to make haste and come when I could join the church for myself.

It was on a Thursday night in April of 1949 when I was finally allowed to join the church. I was all of eight years old. The only other person on the mourner's bench that Sunday was Bro. James Robinson, who was 37 at the time, but now is 84 and is still serving on the Usher Board at St. Jude. As always was the case, my family came to church together. They had been a part of the prayer meeting during the worship service. For me, I was going to get back on that mourner's bench in hopes that today they would let me join the church.

That Thursday night, the choir sang as never before. Aunt Mable sang her favorite song, "How I Got Over." There was a special moving of the spirit. Reverend Mosby preached as I had never heard him. I could not wait until the invitation was given so I could join the church. When it came time, I jumped up and ran to Reverend Mosby. It was not a great decision for me to make, I had made up my mind that I wanted to be a Christian ever since I could remember. Nobody had to stand over me and kneel and pray beside me like Sammy Junior's grandmother had to do for him that night. I was ready! I was ready! When the time came, I let them know I was ready.

I will never forget what Reverend Mosby said to me that day. He said to me, "Little Shirley, do you believe in Jesus Christ as your Lord and Savior?" Anticipating what he was going to say — I had heard this so many times as I watched Pastor Mosby take people into the church — the words shot out of my mouth, "Yes, Sir!!!" "Do you believe he died for your sins?" I responded with assurance, "Yes, Sir!" "Do you want to be baptized?" he said to me in almost baby talk. I again shot back, rocking back and forth, "Yes, Sir!!!" Then he said to me, "Are you willing to be governed by the rules of this church which is the Word of God?" I shot back once again, "Yes, Sir!!!" Finally he said, "How long are you willing to trust in Jesus and to live for Him?" With a kind of mature response, I said unfalteringly, "The rest of my life!!!" All the church shouted and exclaimed, "Amen, Amen, Amen!" Amens went up all over the church. There was much shouting and rejoicing at St. Jude that day. As for me, finally I was in the church, something I had wanted all my little life.

CHAPTER IV

SHAPING MY LEADERSHIP CAPABILITIES

Train up a child in the way he should go: and
when he is old, he will not depart from it.
Proverbs 22:6

The home and church were my first experiences in schooling. I learned my initial lessons in leadership in these two hallmark institutions. The home and church were truly my proving ground. After all, I went back and forth from home to church every day The Lord sent. Whether I wanted to be there or not, my grandmother took me to church. I helped her to clean up on Saturdays. I was with her in meetings from Monday to Friday. But while she was carrying me to church, I was learning what it meant to be a leader and at the same time acquiring leadership skills.

I grew up in a family of leaders. My father was a leader. He came home from military duty with all kinds of medals, certificates, and awards. He was a Staff Sergeant in the Army, he was a leader. Aunt Mable was a leader. She took leadership in the choir, she led many of the songs. And, she was an aggressive business woman, she sold insurance for more then twenty-five years. Then of course, my grandmother, Clara McCray, was a born leader. She held almost every position which could be held in the church, except for the position of pastor. And then, some people used to say she was just like a pastor. So, leadership was in my blood.

It is nothing unusual that I should be so endowed with leadership capabilities, especially in the church. I had little exposure to life in the secular part of the world. I only had limited knowledge of other sections of Memphis. I only went downtown with my grandmother to places like Beale Street. It was in the area of Beale Street where all the Negroes had to go to pay their bills. In addition, doctors' offices and dentists were located in the area of Beale Street as well as the Daisy Theater, W. T. Handy Park and other businesses important for Negroes. Of course, in segregated Memphis of my youth, there was no interaction with white people and their world. My early experience in life revolved around the home place at Cummings and South Parkway.

From there, my circle of involvement was with the church, where I lived out the other half of my life. There is where I was exposed to challenges which called forth my leadership capabilities.

When I joined church at St. Jude at eight years of age, it was then that I seized leadership roles. I became the leader of the youth choir. There was no director of the choir prior to my assumption of that position. I became their leader. I would get the children to rocking as they sang their song for morning worship. There was not too much playfulness, the children were well disciplined because parents were strict in those days. For that reason, it did not take too much for me to be the leader of the children's choir.

At the time I joined the church, I became secretary of the Sunday school. As I learned how to serve as secretary, I was given the assignment of reading the minutes of the Sunday school each Sunday morning. I developed a habit of reading the minutes and rocking back and forth as I blurted out the attendance of each class, the banner class, and who had the largest collection for that morning. I read the minutes in quite an animated manner. My voice rose and fell with each word and expression. My little body responded and reverberated with each word and expression. Then, when I began to conclude my task of reading the minutes, I would rock back on my heels and belch out that the minutes were read by "Sis. Shirley McCray, Secretary. Reverend W. H. Mosby, Pastor!"

My leadership capabilities were shaped at the home place at Cummings and South Parkway as it was in church. I suppose I could say that what I learned at home was just as important and forceful as what I learned at church. Home and church interchangeably worked to impact my life. My leadership capabilities at home really took the form of learning to follow. You can never really lead until you learn how to follow. I had to learn this lesson in a very real way at home.

Although I never had the constant, day-to-day up-bringing of a father in our home, I had these two strong-willed women, my grandmother Clara McCray and Aunt Mable Purnell. These were strong women! Strong willed women! They were very disciplined. They had a daily regimen that varied not in the most minuscule manner. They rose early for breakfast. After breakfast, they cleaned the house. Around noon, we had lunch. Throughout the day, my grandmother did her washing and ironing that she took in from white folk to make some money for the two of us. In the evening, she cooked supper for the two of us and we had plenty of food to eat. In spite of the schedule they kept, it seemed that all the responsibilities which had to be attended to in the course of a day were done easily and in an effortless manner.

My aunt showed her strength in the way she carried on in her home. She was married for more than 52 years and carried a very heavy burden in her home, but she never ceased to attend to her responsibilities. She went out everyday to sell insurance and did exceptionally well. That kind of tenacity influenced me and became consonant with my approach to getting a job done, staying with it until it was accomplished.

Playing football and basketball became a fondness of mine very early in life. But the thing which made it so different with me was that I always played with the boys. In fact, there were no girls in my neighborhood. I don't know what made it that way, there just weren't any girls. So, paper dolls, teddy bears, doll babies, and dishes were not in the equation of life for me. And because there were boys in my neighborhood, I found myself playing games that boys played.

One day I was playing football with the neighborhood boys. The game was one of those heated affairs among youngsters. The chill in the Fall air made a football game just the thing for youngsters like us. The football sailing through the crisp air excited our youthful spirits. We paid little attention to the cool breeze which swayed to limbs of trees and caused the leaves to flutter.

I guess because I was the only girl on the yard, the boys on my team seemed to give preference to me — I was their leader. They called on me to be the halfback. I carried the ball and made touchdowns. They really counted on me to win games for them. I suppose that is why I ended up getting tackled. Because of being a young star, the boys on the other team got jealous and wanted to do something to stop me.

Well, on this one particular play, they gave the ball to me to run for the goal. I took the ball and began to run, just like I had done previously. I was really running! I could run like a gazelle, like a graceful race horse streaking along the race track. Hardly any of the boys had my speed, so they could not keep up with me. I became the envy of the yard.

But one day something happened. I had positioned myself for the kick from the other team. I guess the football hung a little too long, giving the other team an opportunity to get positioned to tackle me. I caught the ball cleanly and began to run with it. I was just running, running like that gazelle, that graceful race horse, like one of those star football players you see on television. All of a sudden someone tackled me from the blind side. I never saw who it was. They just came at me like a barrelling freight train. I could hear the rumble of their rushing run and their pounding pace — but I saw no one.

Then it happened! "Wham!" I felt a dull and painful lick which caused me to see nothing but red. My whole body left the ground. I felt myself sailing through the air. It was like an eternity as I sailed suspended through the air. I finally hit the ground. But, as I hit the ground, I hit with my head striking the hard cold ground. That was the last thing I knew. My lights literally went out. I could not see.

When I came to myself, to know what had happened to me, numbing pain held my body captive. I could not explain how I felt, deep and penetrating hurt was all over me. But that was not all I had to cope with. I really could not see. I tried to open my eyes to see. I guess I had them open, but there was no discernible light registering in the pupils of my eyes. I did not scream nor cry aloud, I was the team leader so I had to demonstrate strength and unquestionable leadership characteristics. I had learned that I had to be tough, like my father, my grandmother, and my Aunt Mable.

The boys on my team picked me up and took me to my grandmother. She chastised me and lovingly berated me for playing football with the boys. She said to me, "I told you about playing with those boys." Responding, I pleadingly said to her, "But Mamma, I don't have anybody to play with but them." She said, rather sternly, "Well, you should act like a girl. You should not be out there playing with those boys."

My grandmother really showed that she cared about me, just as she had all my life. There was no discussion about taking me to the doctor or hospital. We were so poor that hospitals and doctors were just not in our vocabulary. Home remedies were the thing back in those days. My grandmother had a home remedy for virtually everything that ailed you. So, she took something which she had prepared from one of her home remedies and wrapped it around my head with the medicine lying across my eyes. I still could not see! I later learned that the optical nerve which controls eyesight is located in the back of the head. That lick had disturbed that nerve in the back of my head.

I remained blinded for several minutes. I could not see anything. I began to become concerned that I might not see again; however, after some minutes had passed, my sight gradually began to appear. One thing about it, I never played football again. I played basketball, and got real good at it.

That incident is memorable, not so much because of my momentary blindness, but because of the demonstrated leadership characteristics which blossomed in a sport which was dominated by all males. They may have been all males on both my team and the opposition, but I was their leader. That is what sticks out in my mind.

The lesson I learned was a most valuable one, even if it came at a great cost. That lesson was that you have to take the ball when it is given you, the ball of life, and run with it. Conditions are not always favorable when the ball is given to you. Quite often, the opposition seems formidable and it appears that you are the only one in the game other than the opposition. I was the only girl in the game with all those boys. I have to confess, there were times when I felt kind of like I was left out. Regardless of that, however, I was in the game and I had to take the ball and run with it and try to make a touchdown if my team was to win. In addition, I had to be prepared to take the licks and knocks and bruises, my team mates were counting on me. Finally, I learned the intrinsic leadership lesson of tenacity, sticking with the task until you accomplished your objective. I held on to that football in spite of the fact that I got hit and almost lost my sight. That was the price I had to pay if I were to win the game for my team. I had to give it my best in spite of the circumstances.

I had learned these leadership characteristics from my grandmother while a little kid. She always told me to be the best I could be. Her voice registered with me early in life, "Make something out of yourself!" She would say, "Grow up and be somebody!" I had watched how she led that household at Cummings and South Parkway. She ran it like a coordinated corporation. She got things done and made things happen. I watched her as she provided leadership at the church, on the trustee board, on the Mother's Board, in fund raising efforts, and as she led the little boys in her all-male Sunday school class. Her voice rang in my little head like a tolling bell calling toilers to labor, a trumpet calling the warrior to battle.

I suppose these influences from home and church were the driving forces which motivated me when I lead the youth choir, wrote the minutes for Sunday school and stood to read every Sunday with much animation. I did not recoil into some shell of fear and trepidation at the call to exercise leadership in the church. At eight years of age, I joined the church after almost begging to do so. I allowed not the grass of indifference to grow underneath my feet when I joined the church, or sit on my proverbial stool of do nothing waiting on someone to ask me to do something so I could grumble and complain that I did not know how. I leapt for the secretaries position in Sunday school. I grabbed that secretary's minute book and wrote the minutes for each Sunday. When I stood to read, I did so in such an assertive manner that one would think I was past grown. I felt a strong surge of confidence within me when I blurted out the reading of the minutes and then proudly reared my head back and said, "Sister Shirley McCray, Secretary, Reverend W. H. Moseby, Pastor." From that time on, I was destined to be a leader in the church, in my home, and in the world.

CHAPTER V

HOW I WAS CULTIVATED TO CARE FOR YOUNG BLACK MALES

God give us men! A time like this demands
Strong minds, great hearts, true faith and ready hands;
Men whom the lust of office does not kill;
Men whom the spoils of office cannot buy;
Men who possess opinions and a will;
Men who have honor — men who will not lie;
Men who can stand before the demagogue
And damn his treacherous flatteries without winking;
Tall men, sun-crowned, who live above the fog
In public duty and in private thinking;
For while the rabble, with their thumb-worn creeds,
Their large professions and their little deeds,
Mingle in selfish strife, lo! Freedom weeps,
Wrong rules the land, and waiting Justice sleeps.
                    Josiah Gilbert Holland, 1819-1881

First impressions are lasting impressions, so goes the maxim. In my life, that maxim proved to be true. My first impression in my home and church was that there was a lot of love and care for the Black male. I owe my career of working with and trying to develop young Black males to those early experiences in my home and church.

Now it may seem a bit awkward to say I learned to care for the Black male at home and church. There were hardly any males in my home, the place of my first memorable experiences. My father was in the military the first years of my life. When he came back from the military, he took up residence in Chicago, the place of my birth. I spent summers with him and his wife, Leontyne, but the majority of my time was spent in Memphis with my grandmother who had lost her husband, my grandfather, in the years after the Yellow Fever Epidemic in Memphis. There really were no men in our household in Memphis. Aunt Mable was married for more than fifty years to the same husband. However, he was only a small influence in my life. Then, my grandmother, Clara McCray, Aunt Mable, and Aunt Courtney Whitfield were strong-willed women. My grandmother had a way of getting anyone to do just about anything she wanted them to do. She was strong-willed. I guess this was the reason she was over so many things in the church at St. Jude. Aunt Mable was just as strong-willed as Mamma. She had to practically carry the whole load in her home. She had to be strong. Then their other sister was strong. I remember her for her food. She could cook. Mamma would not cook my favorite food as often as I liked. But her sister could cook. She cooked all the things I liked to eat. I found myself going to her house often to get some of her food. It was so good.

So, I spent a great deal of time in my early life with and around women, strong-willed women at that. But it was these women who helped to cultivate within me a care and concern for Black males, especially young Black males.

I grew up in a neighborhood where there were no girls. For blocks and blocks, there were no girls for me to play with. So my alternative was to play with the boys. The boys liked to play those games which required force and physical contact, but I played with them because there was no one else to play with.

My grandmother was very protective of me in every respect. I suppose that was the reason she did not want me playing with the boys, so I would not get hurt. But it was from my grandmother that I really trace back my inspiration for working with boys later in life.

At our home church, St. Jude, my grandmother taught Class No. 10 every Sunday. Class No. 10 was an all boys class. I will never forget this. Mamma never failed to get up on Sunday morning to get to church early to teach her class. In all she did during the week, she worked hard at studying her Sunday school lesson so she could be ready for her class. There seemed to be an extraordinary diligence about her when it came to preparing for what seemed to be her sacred task.

When she stood before her class, she taught with a purpose. She was bent on driving home to their boyish minds some very important lessons of life. Mamma was very knowledgeable of the Bible. When she taught the Sunday school lesson, she thoroughly covered the Bible story which pertained to that lesson. But she had a way of shrewdly and effectively weaving into the lesson the morals of life which she knew the young men needed. She talked to them like a mother and father.

From Mamma's efforts in that Sunday school class, I saw results of a phenomenal magnitude. She developed young men who became outstanding and made a great contribution in life. Three of those young men are still in the church at St. Jude — Deacon Rodell Boyd, Deacon William Davis, and Deacon Robert Harrison.

Deacon William Davis has been a tremendous influence in my life. His behavior in life and concern for me came as a result of my grandmother's influence. When we went to church, we stayed all day on Sunday. On one of those Sundays, I wore for the first time a pair of shoes which my grandmother had bought me. They had high heels. I had never worn shoes with high heels. But, because grandmother had bought them for me, I wore them, and wore them with pride.

I strutted about the church all day in those shoes. But about seven o'clock that Sunday evening, my feet had begun to hurt so much so that I thought I would die. I began to cry, and cry, and cry. I needed some kind of relief because my feet were killing me. Mr. Davis came to my rescue. He literally picked me up and began to carry me home, with me crying every step of the way. He carried me in his arms, consoling me and quieting me all the way from St. Jude Baptist Church, which was located on Emerson Street, to our home at Cummings and South Parkway. While he carried me, his voice rose above my wailing and crying from the pain which held captive my feet and said to me, "You ought not try to be grown!" I told him, "I didn't ask for these shoes! Mamma gave me these shoes!" He was not harsh in his words, he was merely trying to show his care and concern. Mr. Davis was the kind of young man my grandmother developed in her Sunday school class. I was impressed with what she did for him, and secretly I suppose I wanted to be like her.

I began to ponder what Mamma was doing with the young men in Sunday school class No 10. She put so much into what she did in that Sunday school class. It seemed as if she were on some kind of mission each Sunday when she went to stand before her class. She worked so hard during the week to prepare for her class. Then, when she stood before them to teach, she pounded the lesson into them so there was no way they could miss what she was trying to get across.

The impressive thing was that few of the young men she taught went wrong. For the most part, they did not grow up doing bad things. In fact, like Deacon Davis, they grew up to become somebody. Deacon Davis became a prominent layman, teaming up with other men like Bro. Paul Brandon in the state convention of which our church is a member, Tennessee Baptist Missionary and Educational Convention. When I looked at the kind of men my grandmother produced out of her Sunday school class, I wanted to be like her.

My grandmother had a sense of the need for strong Black males in American society. She sensed that strong men needed to be developed in order to provide leadership for our people. I could see that she had done that in her son, my father, Walter McCray. She had five children of her own, four of whom were boys. William and Hazel were twins, and then there were Samuel, Robert and my dad, Walter. She raised the boys in such a way that they possessed leadership capabilities. My dad showed that in the medals and citations he brought back from the military. His military uniform was decorated with ribbons and bars, which let me know that he had been a leader in the military.

My grandmother was very protective of the men in her life, men who came around us when I was a child. I saw this in the way she took care of and protected our pastor, Reverend W. H. Mosby. In the days of my youth, the community held in high honor and respect the preacher, not only Pastor Mosby but every preacher. The preacher was the leader in the Black community as well as the church community. Whenever there was a need to go before the mayor or some city official for an injustice that had been done in the Black community, it was the preacher who took on himself this awesome responsibility. The preacher saw to it that his people got jobs and security. They were concerned with the educational uplift of the young people and the safety of our neighborhoods. Everything that had to do with fund raising for scholarships for young people, the Black preacher took the lead in that enterprise. Then, on Sunday morning they inspired the dispirited masses who came to the church hungering and thirsting for the Word of God.

So, Mamma, like the entire Black community, was very zealous in protecting the preacher. She did not allow any of her household to demonstrate any disrespect or disregard for the preacher. She would not allow anyone to talk about the preacher. For my grandmother, the preacher, Pastor Mosby, any preacher in our community was perfect. He was not God, but he was godly, close to God. She loved the preacher. If the preacher did anything, it was never talked about. If it were talked about, the grown-ups did so in a way that children never heard it or did not know what they were talking about.

I saw first-hand the respect my grandmother had for the preacher. Each Sunday, Pastor Mosby visited one of the member's homes for dinner. That was one of the times I simply hated, because when the preachers came to the house, they ate up everything. When they came to dinner, nothing was left. I wanted to run into the kitchen to get something to eat before they got there because when they came and ate there would not be anything left. That was horrible!

When Pastor Mosby came to dinner on Sunday after church, Mamma cooked all the chicken she had. Now, one thing about my grandmother, she could cook. In fact, all of the three sisters could cook. They were the best cooks in the church. She got up early on Sunday morning frying chicken. The whole house would be filled with the rich aromatic smell of fried chicken. There was something about the smell of fried chicken, a smell that was indescribable. Just the smell made you want to go to the kitchen right then and get a drumstick or thigh and munch on it till your soul and stomach were satisfied. But, this was Sunday and Pastor Mosby was coming to dinner and we all knew that he was going to eat up everything and possibly would not leave anything for us, especially the children.

After church on this particular Sunday, we all came home to prepare for the preacher's coming. On this Sunday, Pastor Mosby brought another preacher with him. I knew we were done for then. When he got to the house, my grandmother made us children go to another room. We were to wait in that room until the grown folk got through eating. If there was anything left, we could have that.

From the room where we were, we could see into the room Mamma used for the dining room. We took turns peeking through the key hole in the door, hoping they would not be so hungry that Sunday so they would leave some for us. Apparently, the preachers had not eaten in quite a while because they dove into that plate of chicken with forks flying. They were laughing and busting their sides about things we did not think were funny. There was joy for them in the dining room, but in our room we were sad and somber. The chicken was disappearing rapidly with no hopes of us getting any at all. Pastor Mosby had a way of placing a large cloth napkin across his chest so grease would not get on his shirt. The other preacher did something similar. But neither one let their daintiness deter them from devouring that platter of fried chicken. A pile of chicken bones steadily rose and their bellies grew larger.

We children took turns peeking through the key hole in the door to monitor the status of the chicken, to see if there would any left for us. When Pastor Mosby got to that last drumstick, panic gripped our room. We could not scream out our displeasure like we wanted to. We just fell back in disgust that all the chicken was gone and we would not have any for ourselves. When the preachers left for the evening, we somberly wandered out into the kitchen surveying the table in the eating room to see if even some crumbs were left. To our dismay, there was nothing. We satisfied ourselves by scraping up something of the leftovers. We could not be angry with Mamma, after all we did get something to eat and we did not end the day hungry. Deep in our hearts as well, we knew the preacher had to be fed.

It was this kind of experience that taught me the supreme respect and lofty appreciation my grandmother had for the preacher, the leader of our community. There was some unwritten law in my family which venerated the Black male among us. There was something special about the Black male. Nurture them, teach them, protect them, this was the unwritten law of my upbringing. And this unwritten law was not limited to the preachers, who were the primary leaders of our community. This law covered all males, regardless of who they were and in what condition they might have been because they might come to occupy some leadership position which could help the Negro Race.

From a very early age, it became soldered into my mind that if our Race was to be great there had to be male power, intelligent and spirit-filled male power. Implicitly, there was something in my mind which instructed me of a dastardly thing that had been done to Black males — of which I was to learn later was the lingering evil effects of American Slavery. Some turbid emotion let me not rest and kept me probing for the cause of whatever the problem was that I saw implicitly present in my neighborhood in South Memphis. The problem was a strange affliction which had been placed upon our Black males. Something had to be done to cure Black males of this malady and crippling affliction. Even then, as early as eight years old when I joined the church, I wanted to do something about this problem. I had seen how my grandmother influenced the young males in her Sunday school class. Unconsciously, I knew I wanted to do something similar. As I look back on my life then, I know now that by God's divine design, He was getting me ready in my grandmother's house and under her influence to do some great thing for the uplift of Black young men.

BOOK II

CHAPTER VI

TRANSITIONS: MY MOVE FROM MEMPHIS TO CHICAGO

Behold, the angel of the Lord appeareth to
Joseph in a dream, saying, Arise, and take
the young child and his mother, and flee into
E'gypt; and be thou there until I bring thee word.
Matthew 2:13

I was born in Chicago, Illinois but I experienced most of my life in Memphis, Tennessee. Nine months out of a year, I spent in Memphis, where my life was really shaped. I spent summers in Chicago with my father. Chicago, however, left a very real impact on my life. Memphis prepared me for the time I spent in Chicago. I received all my school experience in Memphis. By the time I attended school for nine months, I was ready for a change and an opportunity to spend time with my father and the rest of my family. I went to one school throughout my elementary and secondary educational career, from the first through the twelfth grade. Hamilton was the school which gave my educational foundation from the first to the twelfth grade. The school was located at 1478 Wilson Street, sitting at the corner of Wilson and Ethlyn Streets. It sits at that corner to this day, however, it now only serves elementary school grades. Some of those who taught me in elementary school are yet living. Mrs. Thrift Green, who taught me in the 3rd, 4th, and 5th grades, is alive to this day. My 6th grade teacher, Mrs. Holmes, still lives. All these teachers made an indelible impression on me as a little girl.

My elementary school teachers showed me the kind of love, care, concern, togetherness, warmth and family characteristics I experienced at home. I believe it was for this reason that learning was so easy for me. My grandmother constantly reminded me of the need to go further in life, to pursue an educational level beyond anything their generation had ever known. Sometimes she whispered to me while sitting in church. Other times she talked openly and vocally at the dinner table and said, I should go to school, love God, and grow up to make something out of myself. My grandmother made my home environment so positive and strong that it became a natural inclination for me to want to work hard to become somebody as I ventured out into the world. At Hamilton School, the likes of Mrs. Green and Mrs. Holmes were the kind of "mother-like," and "grandmother-like" personalities who made you want to make something out of yourself.

Junior High School and Senior High School were experienced at Hamilton as well. It was there where I began to play basketball in some organized way. Memphis Public schools had not made provisions for girls to play organized league games like basketball. They had league play only for boys in both basketball and football.

In the 7th, 8th, and 9th grades, I played basketball at school. However, because they did not have a team for girls, they made allowance for me to practice with the boys. Throughout Junior High School, the coach of the boys team made an exception for me. In this way, I developed a great many skills for the game which served me well later in high school.

Pick up games in the neighborhood also gave me access to skills which served me well later in life. I played with the boys in our neighborhood. I had to do this because there were no girls to play with. But in playing with the boys, I became as good or better than any of them. In fact, every sport I played, whether it was softball, or basketball, I out played them all.

When we played basketball in the neighborhood, we were forced to make innovations to meet our needs. Our meager resources forced us to construct a basketball goal in order to get our games going. A spent fruit basket or retired vegetable basket served our needs quite well. We cut out the bottom of the willing basket and nailed it to a waiting light pole. This became our basketball goal, the street or the naked dirt was our unmarked court. We chose up team members and played all afternoon and into the evening, A great deal of sweat, set shots; grunts, groans, and jump shots; elbows, energy, and enthusiasm were spent on that spot. When dusk began to fall, we scurried home because parents demanded that their children had to be at home when night fell.

Sports was a clear and central part of my life while growing up in Memphis. However, it did not displace my interest in and concern for my academic performance. My grandmother's voice rang incessantly in my ears, "Go to school . . . Make something out of yourself." Her voice was that of a trumpet sounding one to prepare for war, the beat of an Eternal Drummer coercing and compelling one to abide in the path to certain destiny. Constantly on my mind was the fact that if I did not complete school and make something of myself, there would be no sports, at least in any way other than pick up games in sandlot play and neighborhood gymnasiums. I wanted more than that; so, I studied hard at my lessons so I could get through my classes. I felt this was the door that led to excellence in sports.

High school graduation from Hamilton was a delightful fulfillment of my wildest expectations. My adrenaline ran rapidly as the time drew near for me to march and get my high school sheepskin. So many things converged upon me to enhance the excitement which seized me. I was a member of the largest class to graduate from Hamilton High School and to don its colors of blue and white. Simply to graduate was something my grandmother prayed to lived to see. This in itself was reason enough to be excited.   But there was more. I was awarded several citations and honors for outstanding accomplishments while in school. I was given an award for perfect attendance at Hamilton School from the first to twelfth grades. I felt very proud of myself for this accomplishment. I had decided early in life that I wanted to go to school. I thought if I missed a day at school, I would miss some important lesson about life. So, I developed a love for school, a longing to be there. Because I strove to be the best in everything, I was awarded a citation for being the best female athlete.

The excitement for graduation was further driven by the fact that I was programmed to deliver a speech during the commencement services. And true enough, I delivered a speech on citizenship; and, when I finished, I received a standing ovation from the thronging crowd which had gathered in the gymnasium. Finally, because of my abilities as a vocalist, I was awarded a scholarship in music at S. A. Owen Junior College in Memphis. Although I received the scholarship, I did not attend the school. But, high school was a time of much excitement for me. It was, at that time, one of the mountain top experiences of my life.

My family had not accomplished much in the sense of academics. High school was the farthest most of them had gone in education. I wanted to keep up that kind of family tradition. I had done this and in addition had achieved a status of notoriety with the accolades, citations, and awards I received. But, I wanted to go farther.

At the time of my graduation from high school, one course for my life emerged with graphic clarity. The day following my graduation, my grandmother became terribly sick. As we pondered her condition, ultimately my father decided that the both of us must go to Chicago with him and live. We departed immediately following graduation, travelling all that distance up highway 51 in my father's Ford automobile. What normally was my Chicago hiatus for the summer became permanent relocation, with my grandmother joining me. So, in the summer of 1959, the two of us, Clara McCray and her inseparable granddaughter, Shirley, moved to Chicago.

We first lived with my father at 41st and Drexel. This location only provided a home for us for a brief time. We then moved to live with my father's brother, Samuel, and his wife. They lived at 43rd and Berkley. The south side of Chicago had become familiar to me. When I came to town each summer in past years, I lived with my father on Drexel. Then, I went back home to Memphis. I really never got to experience the entire city itself. I had not experienced the early onset of Fall, the bitter cold of winter, and the protracted blooming of spring. But now, I was getting a full compliment of Carl Sandburg's "Wheat stacker," "Hog butcher" and "broad shoulder" city of the world. For the next two years, Chicago, the city which gave birth to me and so many outstanding personalities in Gospel music, blues, and jazz, would be my home. The city was breath-taking. The skyline of downtown, even then, was towering. Memphis had no skyscrapers, towering, multi-tiered buildings which pointed themselves like giant fingers caressing the sky. Memphis had short, snappy and cold winters. Most of our days in the Queen city of the Mississippi River, the Cotton Capital of the world, were spent under sunlit skies, sometimes with fluffy clouds floating softly overhead.

But, Chicago was different. Chicago's skyscrapers could be seen from afar. They rose up so high that their heads penetrated the dark clouds and mist which frequently bent down so far as to touch the earth. If you looked closely, those tall buildings seemed to gently sway from the stiff wind that came gusting off the giant lake which lay to the east of the shoreline of this enormous city.

Chicago's streets were long and never-ending. They were straight, monotonously straight. And, the people, there were so many. Enormous crowds of people lined the streets, especially at bus stops and train stations which served the elevated trains. I never saw such crowds of people in Memphis. In addition, the crowds were without emotion. The people were without expression. They leaned in the direction of their on-coming bus or train, looking to see if the next car was the one for them to board to their destination. They seemed careful not to say much to the person standing nearby. Chicago presented herself as a not so friendly city.

Public transportation in Chicago, whether on a city bus on the train, was different from anything I had experienced in Memphis. The Memphis I knew was rigidly segregated. That was the case regardless of what you did, segregation was the rule, the law. I can never erase from my mind the humiliation of boarding the bus for a ride to downtown Memphis and having to stand up in the back. The bus, crowded with Negro people getting off from work, was oppressively full in the back, with people standing in the aisle stuck to each other, while there were seats available in the front of the bus, which were reserved for whites only. But in Chicago, it was different. When I went there each summer, as well as this summer when my grandmother and I made our permanent move, segregation was in evidence. I could tell that the South Side of Chicago seemed to be entirely Negro. That seemed somewhat of an oddity. But when we rode the bus or train, we sat or stood in any part of the vehicle. If white people were on the bus or train, they mingled and mixed with us and anyone else who boarded. One noticeable difference was, nobody seemed to talk while they rode public transportation.

Climatic differences noticeably flaunted themselves before us. In Memphis, Spring time started in April, sometimes even in March. We enjoyed warm and balmy temperatures, winds which were moist and warm. Summers in Memphis started in mid-May. In May, the temperatures soared and sizzled. The breeze from the Mississippi River could not cool the heated currents of air which licked at us with its incendiary tongue and searing rays of sun which bore down from the skies. Summers in Memphis were spent swatting mosquitoes at night and fanning flies by day. It was hot! Sultry hot! Often times, unbearably hot! Sweat, heat, fanning and swatting, that was Memphis.

But Chicago was a different story altogether. In June, fierce cool winds were yet blowing off of Lake Michigan. It was nothing to have a jacket to protect yourself from the piercing winds which blew off that lake. In the Windy City, it would be mid-July before the temperatures actually got to where you could break a sweat.

My grandmother and I became situated and acclimatize in the big city by the shores of Lake Michigan. We settled down in the home of my grandmother's daughter-in-law, Aunt Irene. As my grandmother slowly succumbed to the thief of sickness which robbed her of energy, vitality, and even the will to live, I had the responsibility of making her comfortable as she lay on her bed.

The onset of her illness was caused by the ravages of time and hard work. Her seventy-plus year old frame was conceding to a rendezvous with an eighty year old intersection, and this race on the track of time was taking its toll on the travelling frame. She simply could not take to punishment and pain of life she once endured with astonishing alacrity. I watched this tussle with time with pensive dismay and painfully helpless despair. This was my grandmother, who was the only mother I had ever known. She was the real reason for me pressing on in life to become whatever God would have me become. All of my life, she drilled into me the ethics and morals of life. She taught me everyday the things which were right and the things which were wrong. From the days of my infancy, the two of us were inseparable. I loathed the day when separation came as a driven wedge, creating a chasm, the crossing of which we could not make together.

My transition from Memphis to Chicago was a time for me to strengthen the bond with my father. Previously, we renewed our relationship each summer or when he paid a brief visit to Memphis. Oh, we talked frequently by phone by way of long distance between Memphis and Chicago, but now, we were able to communicate on a day-to-day, face-to-face basis. My father was a good father. He always saw to it that I had clothes and especially the things I needed most for the creature comforts of life. He and his wife faithfully sent me a pair of shoes, a dress, and other items of clothes each year. It was not much, but they wanted to be sure I had at least those items of clothing if I did not have anything else.

Although my grandmother's sickness required me to attend to her more closely, she insisted that I remain faithful to her desire for me to stay with God, go to school, and make something out of myself. Because of her insistence, my arrival in Chicago found me immediately seeking a junior college to which I could go in pursuit of my educational goal. All summer was spent calling to inquire about enrollment requirements at junior colleges in the city. There were two or three to which I visited to secure brochures and pamphlets concerning their programs and enrollment requirements.

I came across this Wilson Junior College on 71st and Normal in Chicago. It was a school which seemed to have exactly what I wanted, so, I enrolled. It offered pre-requisite courses for the Liberal Arts Degree. After studying at the two-year school, you were awarded an Associates of Arts degree.

Those days were very exciting. I looked with great anticipation to attending classes in the Fall of the year. One of the surprises was the cordiality of white students who enrolled in my classes. I had not attended school one day in my life with people of the white race. I had not known too many white people up close and personal. It was not a way of life with me in the South. Memphis simply was not conducive to white people coalescing with Black people. As the saying was in Memphis, "Mr. Crump won't allow that." Mr. Crump was the white mayor of long standing who held tightly in his grasp the destiny of Negro people — in a mode of total segregation. But in Chicago's Wilson Junior College, all of this changed.

My professors were very helpful. They made my course work enjoyable and, most importantly, accessible so I could learn easily. One of my professors went to the extent of providing financial assistance when I prepared to graduate from Memphis State University. But the most notable development in my life was the friendships which developed with the students. I still hold friendship to this day with Doris and Sharon. Amazingly, my friendship with white students grew in such a way that it appeared that I had been around them all my life. Ultimately, our relationship with one another became as though there were no color differences at all. It was as if we were brothers and sisters. For the next two years, I was destined to have the educational experience of my young life.

But in my life, education without salvation was frustration. I could never expect to be happy or feel complete without the church in my life in a prominent way. I had grown up in church in Memphis. I had crawled about the church house in my diapers, played in the pastor's spittoon while he preached, and teased the membership with my antics. I had joined the church at 8 years of age, and would have done so earlier had I been given the approval. I became the choir director and leader of the young people in the church very early in my life. I was secretary for the Sunday school and read the minutes with vim and vigor. So, it was only natural for me to be in church.

In Chicago, the church my family attended was Pilgrim Baptist Church. This church was located at the corner of 33rd and Indiana. Serving as pastor was the eminent and nationally known Dr. J. C. Austin. He was well known within the National Baptist Convention, USA, Inc. It was to this church that I went during my summer visits. And now as a teenager, I chose it as my home church after relocating to the Windy City by Lake Michigan.

Church life in Chicago was dynamic and intensive. I suppose there was a desperate need for such spiritual dynamic and intensity. Chicago of the 20s, 30s, 40s, and 50s had become a refuge for hundreds of thousands of Negroes who were escaping the rape and robbery of slavery, emasculation of the plantation, and the humiliation of Jim Crow in the South. It was amazingly unavoidable to notice that those Negroes who fled the South and its oppression, settled on the "south side" of Chicago. I often wondered if the two had some relationship.

The flats, small bungalows, and apartments of South Side Chicago were crowded with hundreds and thousands of Negroes from Mississippi, Arkansas, Alabama and Tennessee. The rabid racism of the South had inflicted the bowels of that part of the nation with severe gastric indigestion and caused it to vomit its poor and pitiful Ebony sons and daughters onto this merciful metropolis of Chicago. But

Chicago presented its own kind of problems. Crowded quarters, lack of education and qualification to pursue high level jobs, and the city's own kind of implicit racism which ran itself out in the fable manner of Blacks being the last hired and first fired, led the Negro to a state of constant anxiety and uncertainty. Living on the plantation in the south or in a small town or city was one thing; it entailed harsh treatment from a mean plantation owner and his overseers, but also there was a slow life-style which afforded some space to stretch and breath. But in Chicago, there was hardly room to stretch or breath. Though this megacity was celebrated as the Promise Land for our people, the paucity of plenty, the emptiness of employment, the madness of materialism, and the unreasonableness of racism were all like fire underneath the feet. In such a crowded condition, such a fire underneath the feet caused Negroes to either turn on and against one another in fear and fighting or turn toward one another in friendship and The Faith. The church for me, Pilgrim Baptist Church, was the place I chose to turn to my people as friends and to Jesus My Lord to strengthen my Faith.

CHAPTER VII

CHICAGO: MY LIFE TOUCHED BY IMMORTALS

Lives of great men all remind us
We can make our lives sublime,
And, departing, leave behind us
Footprints on the sands of time.

Footprints, that perhaps another,
Sailing o'er life's solemn main,
A forlorn and shipwrecked brother,
Seeing, shall take heart again.

The Psalm of Life
Henry Wadsworth Longfellow

Two years is a short period in one's life. But in two years, you can experience that which will shape your life forever. In a brief span of time, one can ascend to the very portals of paradise and be touched by hands immortal. So it was with my experience in Chicago.

Summers spent in Chicago were filled with rare experiences with my father. I cherished each moment we spent together. He was such a positive and powerful force in my life. Each summer, he took me on jobs where he taught me the importance of honest, hard work. I went with him on jobs where we installed plumbing and made plumbing repairs. I assisted him in the repair of automobiles. I also accompanied him when he went to clean up buildings, which included cleaning and freshening toilets. There were not too many jobs we did not perform. I was with him whenever he went to any of them.

He also taught me the skill of work, how to perform a task in such a way that you will be proud of what you have done. His thinking was that if you performed your work notably so that your standards were satisfied, surely the ones for whom you worked would be satisfied. That was a profound lesson for me to learn early in life. It never left me. As a result of what my father taught me in the world of work, I became my greatest critic. I always wanted to perform at my best. I wanted to do whatever I did in such a way that I was satisfied.

But my father, being the great teacher he was, constantly reminded me that the reason for teaching me as he did was his way of getting me to see the need to do something different, to rise above the ordinary, the huddled herd which scuffled for a living among the crumbs of life. His thinking was that if I cleaned enough toilets, got greasy enough repairing cars, was dissatisfied with a meager wage at the close of a week, that would be reason enough for me not to want to choose such a career. I really, really got the message. Those summers I spent previously were not enough to drive home my daddy's lesson. When I came to live for those two years, I really, really got the message. He worked me until I determined in my own mind that was not the kind of career I wanted. His method of teaching reinforced what my grandmother had taught all my life, "Go to school, love God and go to church, and be somebody."

Once I located Wilson Junior College, I made plans to attend. It was located at 71st and Normal and was at that time on the same campus of Chicago Teachers College. When I began my classes and made the necessary adjustments to college life, I discovered that the principles of diligence and hard work my grandmother and father had taught me all my life worked there as well. I cannot say that college life was not difficult, a breeze, but I can say I made it without succumbing to the rigors and stress which others could not handle. I graduated from Wilson in two years.

Some of my greatest experiences in Chicago occurred in the church. Pilgrim Baptist Church became the center of my life once I arrived in Chicago. It was in this church's environment that I came under the influence of one of the world's greatest spirits, Mr. Thomas A. Dorsey.

Meeting great personalities had not been unknown to me. In Memphis, I had the privilege of meeting the great Ms. Lucy E. Campbell. She was like a household name. Dr. W. Herbert Brewster's church, East Trigg Baptist Church, was not far from where we lived. As I progressed in my singing career, we often visited his church and met Ms. Queen C. Anderson. She was the vocalist who made popular many of the songs Dr. Brewster wrote. Dr. Brewster himself was an affable personality, dapper in his dress as a Baptist preacher. Towering in his physical presence, he took on the angelic image of Gabriel fresh from the realm of heaven.

Also in Memphis, I had the rare privilege of meeting Ms. Mahalia Jackson. She was one of my favorite singers. I just loved to hear her ring out the harmonies of heaven with her melodic voice. She came to Memphis to give a Mother's Day concert at Ellis Auditorium. The auditorium was filled to capacity, but I was successful in getting close enough to meet her.

Her face was round, taking on the appearance of a brown cherub. Her hair was artistically curled about her head, an arrangement which clad her in the natural apparel of serenity. She was simply dressed, but obviously adorned with clothes of a costly kind. Most impressive was her manner of speech to me. She was cordial and warm. Her warm eyes drew me to herself. We engaged in a conversation of pleasantness. My departure from her left me with the feeling of having been kissed by the zephyrs if heaven itself.

So, when I got to Chicago, I was not impoverished of experiences of meeting some of the greats in the field of music. But Chicago provided me the opportunity of promenading onto the field of the truly greats and consorting with them in musical intimacies.

The first Sunday after I arrived in Chicago, I joined Pilgrim Baptist Church. Pilgrim was the home church of the world renown Mr. Thomas A. Dorsey. The church was not in walking distance from where we lived. It was located at 33rd and Indiana and we lived at 43rd and Berkley. So, we either rode the bus to church on Sunday, or someone from the church came to pick us up and carry us to worship. Pilgrim had a large congregation. It was not like St. Jude in Memphis. There, you knew everyone and everyone knew you. But at Pilgrim, the congregation was so large that it was unlikely that you would know all the people who attended. But soon I became known. At first, I was known as Mrs. Pierce's cousin. Mrs. Pierce was Aunt Mable's daughter. Others knew me as Mrs. McCray's niece and Mr. McCray's daughter.

The second Sunday after I joined the church, I joined the choir. I joined both the youth chorale and senior choir. Pastor Austin learned that I could sing, so he began to request that I sing a solo or lead the choir in singing. To the membership of Pilgrim Baptist Church, I became "Little Shirley."

Very soon after joining the church, the youth chorale and senior choirs, I came under the influence of Mr. Thomas A. Dorsey. When I went to Pilgrim, Mr. Dorsey was at least in his late sixties or early seventies. He lived to be so much older, maybe even reaching a hundred.

I watched as he came into the church with his very weak frame. Sometimes, he had to be helped into the church. Entrance into Pilgrim was a rather arduous affair. The sanctuary was elevated high above ground level. There were high steps which members had to negotiate in order to get to the sanctuary. Sometimes, some of the members had to assist Mr. Dorsey to get up those stairs. But, once in the sanctuary and in the choir stand, he sat in his appointed seat in the choir stand, a location which had been his for many years.

When time came for Mr. Dorsey to lead a song or direct his choir, he rose to take his position on a pedestal. He was strict about his music. When he stood before his choir, he expected everyone to pay attention to him. He liked his music played a certain way. Because he was so peculiar about his music, there was only one person he preferred to play for him and his choirs. Sis. Julia Washington was that person. She was the only musician who played to satisfy Mr. Dorsey. She was a great singer also. She did solo work which caused angels to blush.

Mr. Dorsey's manner of directing his choir was by wielding his celebrated one finger. He used that one finger of his to wring from every member of his choir the sweetest music, music which moved the soul toward heaven. When Mr. Dorsey was ready, when he stood before his choir, he looked intently at each member in the choir stand, demanding their most scrutinizing attention. Once he was satisfied that all eyes were on him, he raised his celebrated one finger. Once his finger was raised, Sis. Washington struck the piano chord leading into the song. The music of Thomas A. Dorsey was then underway. Each beat was orchestrated by that one finger. When his one finger came down, the choir hit its note.

I was privileged to join the Youth Gospel Choir, which was also under the direction of Mr. Dorsey. This is the group which travelled on concert tours, under the leadership of Mr. Dorsey. Through this experience, I became very close to Mr. Dorsey. I became a member of the National Gospel Singer's Association, of which Mr. Dorsey was founder. As a member of the Youth Gospel Choir and the National Gospel Singer's Association, under Mr. Dorsey's leadership, we toured cities located mostly in the northern hemisphere of the United States.

Mr. Dorsey's house was a natural gathering place for rehearsals for Gospel Singers. I was there as frequently as I was anywhere else in Chicago. While visiting Mr. Dorsey's home for engagement in rehearsals, I met the renown Sallie Martin, founder of the famed Sallie Martin Singers. Ms. Martin was, like Mr. Dorsey, a very strict person when it came to her music. If she said for you to do something, she meant for you to do it. So many other Gospel music celebrities frequented Mr. Dorsey's home, coming and going as casually as the passing of a day.

I enjoyed the rare privilege of hearing the pristine versions of Mr. Dorsey's most popular songs. With his feeble voice, I heard him sing,

I am tired and so weary,
But I must toil on,

46

Till the Lord comes to carry me away.
Where the morning is bright
And the Lamb is the light
And the night is as fair as the day.

There will be peace in the valley,
for me, some day.
There will be peace in the valley,
for me, O Lord I pray.
There'll be no sadness, or sorrow,
no trouble I'll see.
There will be peace in the valley
for me.

Many are the times I heard him tell the story which led to the writing of his memorable, *"Precious Lord, Take My Hand."* His story was that he lost his wife to sickness and death and likewise his child. When he thought he could not carry on any further, he implored the Lord to lead him through that stormy period of his life.

Precious Lord, take my hand
Lead me on, let me stand.
I am tired, I am weak, I am worn,
Through the storm, through the night,
Lead me on to the light,
Take my hand, Precious Lord, lead me on.

When my way grows drear,
Precious Lord, linger near.
When my way is almost gone,
Hear my cry, hear my call,
Hold my hand, lest I fall.
Take my hand, Precious Lord, lead me on.

When the darkness appears,
And the night draws near,
When my day is passed and gone.
At the river, here I stand,
Guide my feet, hold my hand,
Take my hand, Precious Lord, lead me on.

When Mr. Dorsey had grown feeble and many years were resting heavily upon his head, many of the Gospel music celebrities, led by

Ms. Sallie Martin and the Sallie Martin Singers, came to Pilgrim Baptist Church and did a commentary on his life and his music.

Being at Pilgrim Baptist Church for that period in my life was indeed a great experience. I could not have had a greater person to influence my life than that of the personality of Mr. Thomas A. Dorsey. Under his tutelage, so many things of musical magnitude were brought out of me. It was like being in the presence of The Great Musical Sculptor Himself, the Lord God Almighty. Certainly, Mr. Dorsey was not God, but in his own way, he was God's representative in the sense of music. His music had a way of lifting the soul to God. His music had the power to propel one's soul from the miry bog of this world's misery, to leave that mire and bog with all its hellish stench to hotly pursue the heights of heaven and a rendezvous with the God of the universe. The south side of Chicago with its harsh conditions of life, the milling of millions of men, masses marching to and fro to plants and places of work, folk wide-eyed with anxious engagement in fierce competition in the factory and fields of forced labor, caused the human spirit to look for some otherworldly resolution. Hence, Mr. Dorsey helped the soul engage in this hunt for heaven when he musically averred that "There will be peace in the valley, some day."

My Chicago experience was indelibly etched on the tablet of my mind, spirit, and body. It seemed as though God Himself, working through the hands of men and women in the sphere of my life on the south side of Chicago, took my mind, spirit and body in the palm of His Eternal Hands. As such, I felt I had been molded for some divine purpose in the world. God Himself, through the immortals whom I encountered during my sojourn in the great Windy City, sculpted my life, my mind, my spirit, my entire being. I had had a rendezvous with immortals. I could never be the same.

It really was incredible what had happened to me in my Chicago experience. It was something similar to what I had read of Paul the Apostle when he had his experience of being elevated to the third heaven. He reported to the Corinthians that in his ethereal experience, he heard things which he could not report and beheld things which were too powerfully sacred for the human tongue to tell. As I interacted with Mr. Thomas A. Dorsey, Ms. Sallie Martin, and the greats of the world of the church and Gospel music, I concede that the experience is so powerful that it is difficult for my human vocabulary to express what I have beheld. I do know this, my life was touched by immortals.

CHAPTER VIII

THE DEATH OF MY GRANDMOTHER

Be still, sad heart! and cease repining;
Behind the clouds is the sun still shining:
Thy fate is the common fate of all:
Into each life some rain must fall,
Some days must be dark and dreary.
The Rainy Day
Henry Wadsworth Longfellow

The words of the poet could never be truer. Into my life the rain of sadness and loss was to fall, cascading into waves, yea, torrents of utter despair. The end of the life of my grandmother was drawing nigh.

For two years I had enjoyed the glamour and glory of basking under the starlit sky of Chicago's world of celebrities. I had been touched by the immortal life of the truly greats in the world of music, Thomas A. Dorsey and Sallie Martin to name only a few. I was in a state of euphoria, truly a state of ecstasy. I had stood on the sun drenched summit of success, as far as interaction between a lowly Memphian and Chicago's stellar performers in the world of Gospel Music was concerned. But now, life was preparing me for a startling blow which would set me into a free fall toward the pit of utter despair.

I was winding up my two years at Wilson Junior College. There were only a few months left before graduation in June of 1962. My course work was progressing well. There was no foreseeable problem to prevent me from receiving my diploma. However, a sudden development caused the earth to shake with a turbid quake. My grandmother's illness grew more grave. She had been stricken in Memphis, so much that she was unable to carry on her natural duties of running the home place as she had done for so many years. Her illness was the reason for us moving to Chicago. Though in Chicago, my grandmother really had never left Memphis. She loved Memphis. She loved St. Jude. In fact, she insisted that she did not want to die in Chicago. She let us all know that she wanted to die in Memphis. She was so much of a believer in the Bible and an emulator of its sainted characters that she wanted to be like the Old Testament Patriarch, Jacob, and Joseph his son. They did not want to be buried in Egypt. Mamma went even a step further, she did not want to die in the "Egypt" of her circumstance, Chicago.

As I was seriously considering my studies at the college, in preparation for the last round of papers and tests I had to accomplish before graduating, my grandmother announced that she did not think her time was long. Simultaneously, she registered her request for my father and I to carry her back to Memphis where, whenever God called, she would be ready to go. My grandmother had spoken, who could have the audacity to fail to respond.

I knew this day was coming, but, I suppose like so many things in life which you feel will never happen, I was hoping against hope that my grandmother's sickness would not be unto death. The mortality of mankind was not something I had taken well to in life. Moreover, my grandmother and I had cultivated such an inseparable bond. Whenever you saw one of us, you generally saw the other. She carried me to church and we were together there. As I grew up, she carried me with her to clean the church building on Saturday. I was always with her in all of her auxiliary meetings during the week. People knew us as one. It was unthinkable for me to leave her in Memphis when I made preparations to go to Chicago for the summer after graduating from high school. So, when she suddenly got sick and my dad insisted that we pack her things and bring her along, I eagerly consented. We had to be together all the years of my life! Now, I had to get use to the thought of us not being together for the rest of my life.

The days seemed to lengthen with painful protraction. Each day leading to our departure for Memphis seemed never to end. My grandmother seemed already to have made a mental and spiritual transition to another setting. Her sickness was borne with much pain and anguish, but her mind and spirit seemed to be at peace with God, as if she had already had a visit by His Divine Presence, lifting her to the Ultimate Realm of Righteousness where the wicked cease from their troubling and the weary are at rest. I could hardly bear it. She was in pain and anguish physically, but in her spirit, she was already at rest.

I thought I was strong. I gladly moved her from the bed to a comfortable sitting place in her room. Without complaint, I changed her bed linen and tried to make her as comfortable as possible. I was willing to do anything to help her cope with her illness. I did everything possible to help her do so. But, I was not willing, at least I did not want to let her go take death's journey to the grave. This thought troubled me so.

Hoping against hope as I might, the thing I hoped for did not come to pass. My hope was that I might have my grandmother forever in life; that simply was not to be. She finally succumbed to the forces of finality and persuaded us to take her back to Memphis where she could live out her last days.

My father and I made preparations for the journey. We packed my grandmothers belongings in the Ford, the car my father loved to drive. He only loved to drive Fords. When we were ready, we took to the highway, going south to Memphis. The drive was long, much longer than our trip two years ago. I thought that trip was long. The two lane highways we travelled were so congested. We went through towns where traffic sometimes was at a standstill or moved at a snail's pace. The ride down highway 51 seemed twice as long as the trip two years prior. It seemed as though there was a little town every fifteen miles. In every town, cars were in abundance. Bumper to bumper they stood at each intersection of every village and town. This was the way the trip went all the way from the south side of Chicago to the south side of Memphis.

After we traveled for what seemed to be an eternity, we finally arrived at Memphis. But this trip back home, was so very, very different. It was one in which there would be a final farewell to the one who had meant all the world to me, my grandmother.

The sad arrival finally came. At least we were relieved of the constant bumping and jostling from riding in a car engaged in perpetual motion for hour after hour. You do not know how good it feels being able to sit in a comfortable chair in a house until you have been bounced about in an uncomfortable automobile for hundreds of miles. Arriving in Memphis, we made our way to the home place at the corner of Cummings and Parkway. With assistance from family members, we took my grandmother from my father's automobile and transported her to her bedroom where we made her as comfortable as we could.

I was still in school, looking forward to graduating from Wilson Junior College — something my grandmother prayed that God would allow to happen. I looked forward to graduating, but not without my grandmother's presence. The thought of her not being present at my graduation kept the clouds of sadness hanging precipitously low over my head continuously. Because of my pending graduation, my father and I had to return immediately to Chicago. But, this was not something easy for me to do. When it came time for us to depart, a strong and compelling feeling began to tug at my soul, preventing me, pulling me back, not allowing me to move in the direction of my father's automobile. I became overwhelmed with despair. Tears flooded my eyes. I cried uncontrollably. My grandmother and I hugged and embraced for moments we never wanted to end. Like the time my lights were put out from a deadly blow on the neighborhood lot when someone tackled me, so another kind of deadly blow had hit me, blinding me so I could not see through blurry tears which flooded my eyes and the piercing pain which broke my heart.

My father gently pulled at my arm, gesturing that we needed to leave. But I could not bring myself to say "goodbye" to my grandmother. Lurking in the back of my mind was the horrid thought that this could be the last time I would see her in life. I did not want it to happen. It could not happen. My grandmother could not leave me, we were inseparable. How could I get along in life without her?

These questions flooded my mind like the tears which flooded my eyes. I could not think clearly. Unanswered questions, yea, unanswerable questions careened about in the chambers of my mind. The sound of their inquiry and quest for attention muffled out my father's call and command for us to be on our way back to Chicago. I finally conceded to the inevitable. With eyes aflood with tears and a heart breaking with sorrow, I went back to my grandmother and took her once again in my arms and hugged her with all the might I had, or such as I could apply to her frail and emaciated body. I whispered to her, "I love you mamma! We will be praying for you! Take care of yourself!" Having said that, my father and I went for the door, resisting the temptation of looking back at the one who meant so much to us.

The ride back to Chicago was uneventful. It seemed to be twice as long as any trip we had made previously, whether to Chicago or to Memphis. There was not a lot of talk between my father and I, our minds seemed to be completely preoccupied with thoughts of his mother, my grandmother.

Sure enough, only a few days passed before we got the dreaded call that my grandmother had died. Once again, I lost control of my emotions. As Jesus wept over the one whom he loved, Lazarus of the little village of Bethany, I wept over the death of the one whom I loved, my grandmother, Clara Dean McCray. She was gone! My father and all the family in Chicago began to make arrangements for the trip back to Memphis for the funeral.

Of course, the funeral was held at St. Jude Baptist Church, the church of which she had a part in bringing into existence. She had given her life to that church. It is little wonder why she wanted to be in Memphis when it was time to fall asleep in Jesus' arms. She wanted to be at home at St. Jude.

St. Jude and the entire immediate neighborhood and community paid highest respects to this sainted woman, a woman of women. Her life, spent well and lived to a ripe old age, was replete with fruit from her labors. Her sons from Sunday school classes over the years came to bid farewell. The preachers who graced her table and sated their palates with crisp fried chicken came to launch their loquacious lips in plenteous praise. All the auxiliaries to which my grandmother belonged were represented at the funeral. They all read their resolutions, which rang with glowing words of accolades and panegyrics. Then came the sermon. It would be the last time Clara Dean McCray would be in the presence of a sermon delivered from the pulpit of St. Jude Baptist Church. And, the funeral would be the final Sunday school lesson she would teach. The Motto Text would probably be:

> Blessed are the dead which die in the Lord
> from henceforth: Yea, saith the Spirit,
> that they may rest from their labours; and
> their works do follow them.
> Rev. 14:13.

Life without Clara Dean McCray was indescribable. The void was inexpressible. The pain from the loss was unbearable. But, life of necessity had to go on. So, we returned to Chicago with the intention of somehow allowing life to go on. I returned to school at Wilson Junior College. I had to live under the awful feeling of not having my grandmother to witness the ceremony of my graduation from college. This was something she worked so hard to bring about and longed to see. Wish as I may, Mamma McCray would not be on hand to watch me march at the commencement ceremony.

My graduation from Wilson Junior College was a great achievement for the McCray family. Not one of our family had gone farther than high school. No one had attended college at that time. I was the first in the McCray family to attend college. I was the first in the McCray family to graduate from college, even though this was a two year college. None of my family had ventured this far in the field of academics.

There was another first at work at the commencement ceremony of Wilson Junior College. I was one of the first Blacks to attend this school. In the South, segregation was yet established hard and fast in the early sixties. Defacto segregation was a fact of life. Only in Montgomery, Alabama, Nashville, Tennessee, Greensboro, North Carolina and a few other places had Martin Luther King, Jr., and a few others challenged segregation. In Chicago and in the north, racial exclusion was not so pronounced, but it was there. Wilson Junior College was a case in point. Prior to my coming to the school, there were no Negroes attending. I became a first.

The commencement at Wilson did not charge me with a surge of adrenaline like the Hamilton graduation two years before. The moment of my graduation was made more meaningful by the fact that I had accomplished that for which my grandmother worked so hard and prayed so hard. All during the time of the ceremony, I could hear her voice ringing with distinguishable clarity, "Love God, go to school, and make something out of yourself." In those words, Clara McCray was present on the campus of Wilson Junior College when I graduated. I graduated in June of 1962.

The next six months following my graduation were bland and routine at best. I was in an unstable state. I really did not know what life would be like without my grandmother. Now, I was learning a painfully important lesson — how to carry on without one whom you dearly love. I tried hard to make the adjustment. During the next few months following graduation, I worked during the day while taking some classes at night. After that, I reversed the process and attended some classes during the day while working at night. At one point, I worked from 3:00 p.m. till 9:00 p.m. at a community center and attended some classes during the day. Following that, I worked during the day at a Spiegals Catalogue Company while taking courses at night. Spiegals paid rather handsomely. They paid according to production.

Life for me, however, was becoming circular. It seemed that I was simply going around in circles. I was not getting anywhere or accomplishing anything. More and more each day, I could hear the voice of my grandmother loudly challenging me to "Love God, go to school, and make something out of yourself." Her voice haunted me! She stayed ever before me, driving me toward something greater than selling merchandise out of a Spiegal's catalogue.

Finally, I couldn't restrain myself any longer. I was compelled to return to Memphis in pursuit of whatever it was my grandmother thought I should do to make something out of myself. I had no money, but I knew I had to do what I had to do.

I wanted my aunt, Mable Dean Purnell, to know of my desire to return home to Memphis. I wrote her a letter conveying my desire. I finally called by phone and told her that I wanted to return to Memphis. She told me that would be what "Sister" would want. Aunt Mable called my grandmother, "Sister," for indeed the two were sisters. She said, "Sister would want you to finish school." So, she said she would do all she could to help me. She did what she said. She saw to it that I had enough to return home to Memphis. When I had made the necessary arrangements for my departure, and after biding farewell to Pilgrim Baptist Church, my father, and family, I was bound back to the South and the city of Memphis.

CHAPTER IX

MY RETURN TO MEMPHIS

'Mid pleasures and palaces though we may roam,
Be it ever so humble, there's no place like home.
Home, Sweet Home
From the opera Clari, the Maid
of Milan

John Howard Payne

It was January of 1963 when I returned to Memphis. It was cold, but not the bitter cold I had left in Chicago. Things had not change too much. The Mississippi River was still busy with riverboat traffic and Front Street piers were bustling with boats being unloaded of their wares. Main Street was still the central transfer point for everyone riding the trolley system. Hundreds of people stood shivering in the January cold waiting on their trolley.

Segregation still was very much a part of public life. I was forced to become familiar once again with riding the trolley in the back section reserved for Blacks. The only exception was those trolley lines which ran in predominantly Black neighborhoods. But it was nothing to see a trolley filled to capacity in two-thirds of the vehicle, from the back to the front, but with several vacant seats in the very front. That was because although there were no whites on the trolley at the time, that part of the vehicle was reserved for them and Blacks could not sit in those sits no matter what. In spite of racial conditions, this was home and I was glad to be back home.

It was good to see the Beale Street section of downtown Memphis. The south side of Chicago had its appeal to Negro culture, but it was not to be compared with Beale Street. I was thrilled once again to see the Daisy Theater, Handy Park and the statue of the Father of the Blues, W. T. Handy, and to see and hear all the hustle and bustle that took place in the Beale Street area. I knew I was home when I heard the blues spilling out of the windows and doors of taverns which lined Beale Street. Truly it was good to be back home.

One of the first things I did upon arriving back home was to get back into the mainstream of church life at St. Jude. Going back to my home was a bittersweet experience.

It could never be the same without Clara McCray sitting in her usual place on the Mother's Board dressed in all white. I was no longer small enough to crawl about on the floor and play with the pastor's spittoon. All that was missing. But it was good to be back home at St. Jude. It was like being back with my caring, loving, concerned family.

I resumed my place in the choirs of the church. I loved to sing. God had given me a voice and I was bent on using it to His glory. I really emersed myself in the work of the church. I suppose I wanted to reincarnate my grandmother in the sense of trying to do all she did in church, except developing an all male Sunday school class. In virtually ever phase of church life, I tried to take a part.

When I arrived in Memphis, I had no money and no prospects for a job at the moment. I went to live with my Aunt Mable. She had a nice home, well kept and with adequate room for me. She felt it was her responsibility to take care of me now that her sister, Clara McCray, had died. She did more than I could ever expect.

To solve my job problem, my Aunt Mable had called my cousin, Griffin Johnson, and asked him to intercede for me at the place of his work. He worked as a foreman at Bruce's Box Factory in Memphis. Griffin had talked to his boss about giving me an opportunity to work. His boss agreed and hired me to work. So, after I arrived in Memphis, it was confirmed that I had a job. I was so glad to get a job that I set out to be the best at whatever they assigned me to do.

My first day on the job, I showed up early. I had developed a habit of doing that, arriving earlier than the prescribed time. My contention was that it was always better to be where you were supposed to be at the particular time than to be trying to get there. So, I was always at work much earlier than time to clock on the job. Another thing which had become an integral part of the thinking in my life was that of never missing a day on the job. For twelve years at Hamilton school, I developed a habit and noted reputation of never missing a day in school. In fact, they gave me a citation for such an accomplishment. I carried that kind of diligence and discipline with me to Chicago. I would now employ it in the world of work in Memphis.

My assignment at Bruce Box Factory was, making boxes. I put large corrugated boxes together. With a large stapling machine, I stapled boxes together. I tore into the job with a passion. I worked hard at doing a good job. I guess I did such a good job that the boss increased my salary and put me on the 11:00 p.m., to 7:00 a.m. shift. I did not complain about the shift change or the time, I was glad to be working. I could easily adjust my sleeping hours to accommodate night time work. In addition, I was glad to get a raise in pay. I could use the money.

In the process of assembling boxes, I developed a rather rapid pace for performing my work. In fact, I was extremely fast at assembling and stapling those corrugated boxes. One night, the boss came by my work station and, while looking at me do my work, said, "I have never seen anyone work so fast!" I was capable of turning out three or four stacks of boxes per night. That was a lot of boxes.

My work habits were reflective of the training my father gave me while I worked with him in Chicago. He taught me to do any job well. My grandmother taught me to perform any assignment with excellence. So, on this job, I demonstrated well what I had been taught about how to perform in the world of work.

However, working from 11:00 p.m. to 7:00 a.m., did not satisfy me and the hunger for higher things. My grandmother had instilled that in me and it was a part of the fibers of my very being. I was beginning to bring home a decent paycheck, but I was starving my mind and diminishing my spirit. I had to do something about this. There yet was something missing in the equation of life. My grandmother had continued to tell me to "Love God," I was doing that and going to church as much as anyone. But, she told me to "go to school, and make something out of your self." I was not doing that. Finishing Wilson Junior College only partially satisfied that mandate. I needed to do something to complete the equation.

I tried to solve that problem by arranging to take the entrance test for acceptance at Memphis State University. I decided on Memphis State University because of economics. There were at least two other schools I could have considered. Tennessee State University in Nashville was probably my preference. Everyone I knew in Memphis was talking about Tennessee State. That was the school. But Tennessee State University was two hundred miles away and I did not have the finance to make that kind of transition. LeMoyne College was closer, in the heart of South Memphis, but it cost more to attend there than it did to attend Memphis State University. So, Memphis State University was the likely choice for me, even with the probable racial problems I might encounter.

I knew my choice of Memphis State was a bold step because that institution was yet reluctantly yielding to integration. There were only a few Black students who had applied and been accepted as students. The entrance of those few Black students was not without controversy and constant trouble on their part. But, I was determined to apply and, with all that was in me, pass the test to be accepted.

I made every effort to adequately prepare for the test. Try as I did, when time came for me to take the test, I was unsuccessful. I failed the test. I could not believe I was unable to pass such an entrance test, in light of the fact that I had completed Wilson Junior College in Chicago. I thought I really did not have whatever it took to go on to an institution of higher education. I began to have a low opinion of my intellectual capability. Discouragement over took me. It looked as if I was not going to college at Memphis State.

But Aunt Mable met my discouragement with strong, inexorable words of encouragement. She said to me, "Don't you give up. Don't you give up." Her passionate appeal did something for me. It gave me the kind of incentive I needed to overcome the near fatal discouragement that held me in siege. I then realized the test was skewed against people of the ebony hue. The test they set before me reflected hardly any of the things I encountered in my community of Cummings and Parkway. My educational experience at Hamilton was in another world when compared to the world reflected in the test I took at Memphis State University. But still, I had to take that test and pass if I wanted to attend that school. I decided that was what I was going to do.

I engaged my mind in the most serious study and reflection I had ever done. I tried to recall all the areas the test covered. Having done so, I studied in those areas, I read all I could and all I thought I had to read to be ready for the test. I read and studied myself full until I thought I was mentally ready.

In addition to my mental preparation, I began to pray seriously about my condition. I asked Aunt Mable to pray. I asked my church family to pray. We all prayed that God would give me the ability to recall the information I needed to pass the test. We all prayed and prayed. I really prayed hard, asking God for the mental capacity and psychological strength to master the information that would be set before me. My prayers were answered. When I took the test the second time, I passed the test. I was ready to go on to Memphis State University and complete the two years I needed to finish college.

BOOK III

CHAPTER X

INTEGRATING MEMPHIS STATE UNIVERSITY

I'm tired of sailing my little boat,
Far inside the harbor bar;
I want to go out where the big ships float,
Out in the deep, where the great ones are.
And if my frail craft seems to slight,
For waves which sweep these billows o'er,
I'd rather go down in the stirring fight,
Than drowse to death by the blissful shore.
Quotable Quotes of Benjamin Elijah Mays

I entered Memphis State University in the Fall of 1964. Integration was beginning to make its impact on Memphis. That impact was felt on the campus of Memphis State just as it was all over the city of Memphis. Southern whites did not yield easily to integration, and it was painfully felt on the campus of Memphis State. When I entered that school, it was a test of faith of everything I learned in church. My whole being, my mind, my spirit, and my flesh were all tested when I went to that school. Being the only Negro in my classes, it was lonely, the folk were cold, and racism was rigid.

I majored in health and physical education. I was the first Black to enroll in that department as well as the first Black to graduate from that department. I was successful in mastering my studies in spite of the fact that I had failed the first entrance exam I took. I was called "Nigger" so much that I literally got tired of it. I got to the point that I loathed the place and wanted to drop out of school.

I tried to endure the cat calls, the sneering, and racial epithets, being called "Nigger," but it was hard. Many days I returned home to my aunt's house in tears. She asked me, "Why are you crying?" I told her, "Those kids at school keep calling me `Nigger' and they keep messing with me." I told her I was going to drop out of school. But, she kept after me, saying, "You're going to finish! You're going to finish!" I thought I was a go-getter and could take anything and put up with most anything. I had played football with big burley boys and had stood their intimidation and physical punishment. I had excelled in school at Hamilton and had been cited for my excellence. But the rabid racism at Memphis State almost took its toll on me.

I am glad my aunt stayed on me and made me go back to school day after day. I do not know where I would be today or what I would be doing had she not done that. I learned a most profound lesson from that ordeal. If you get learning in the head, no one can take it from you. Also, had I not the strong background in the church, home, and community, I could not have made it. I learned that any Black person who wishes to make something of himself or herself in America must have the strength of the church behind them to make it. Otherwise, they can explode or go crazy. I did neither one. I had my family and my church behind me, reinforcing me and giving me the spiritual strength I needed to fight the battle.

My church family at St. Jude gave me support that can never be forgotten. Everyone at church knew I was in school at Memphis State. Also, they knew I was having a difficult time in every way. A word of encouragement was on the lips of everyone. There were members, like Mrs. Azzie L. Boykins, who walked up to me on Sunday morning and pressed into my hand a piece of money and said,"This is your lunch money." Someone else would come and say to me, "This is your bus fare to get to school." Even the pastor of St. Jude, who has been there now for more then thirty years, Reverend J. S. White, gave me five and ten dollars out of his pocket once a month. They all let me know they were praying for me. This is what carried me through Memphis State University.

My studies were not exceptionally difficult. I knew how to study and get my lessons. I knew I had the ability to achieve in college, if I were given half the chance. My class work did not give me much of a problem. It was when I attempted to penetrate the sports program and become a part of the girl's basketball and volleyball team that I really felt the racial wrath of white people at Memphis State.

As a part of my health and physical education studies in which I was majoring, some of my gym classes involved basketball. I played that game well. In fact, when I graduated from Hamilton High School in 1959, I was honored as the best female athlete by my peers. One of those sports was basketball. I loved that sport. I was really good at it.

One of my gym teachers observed closely my ability to play basketball. She stopped me in the gym one day and said, "Girl, you really are good." She continued, "You ought to come out for the basketball team." I thought much of her idea, not realizing what was in store for me if I really pursued the matter. It simply did not dawn on me the difficulties which lay ahead.

With a good deal of *naïveté* and rather elementary boldness, I went to the girl's basketball team coach, Ms. Elma Roane, and asked if I could be on the team. The first time, she simply said, No!" I went back the second time and asked and her "no" was qualified by the statement that "We don't have any uniforms."

I felt Ms. Roane, the head coach of the girl's team, was very prejudiced. She had one of those southern drawls, and a kind of sneer when she talked. Her lips twisted in a way that communicated contempt for the one to whom she was speaking. She did not speak this way to everyone, I noticed it only when she spoke to me. That's the way I felt then.

I took her rejection of my overture painfully, but as something at the time I could do nothing about. I was fuming that I was not allowed to play basketball for some frivolous reason. One day, one of the white girls on the team, who knew of my interest in playing and who also knew of the coach's rejection of my request to play with the frivolous reason that she did not have a uniform, pressed a note in my hand. She said, "Shirley, I wrote down the days we are going to practice. Put this in your pocket. You come to the practice." I said, "Okay!"

I got my aunt's car that afternoon and drove back to school. I walked into the school and then to the gymnasium where the girls were practicing. When the coach looked and saw me, you could have bought her for a nickel. She did not know I knew there was a basketball practice that day. She looked at me with a quizzical, puzzled look, but never said anything.

I sat on the bench and watched the kids play. They all knew me and knew how well I played basketball. They had seen me in gym class. In fact, some of them were in my gym class. After awhile, some of them came over to me and said, "Come on, Shirley, come on out here and play with us." The coach said nothing, either to consent or deny permission. So I got up from the bench and went onto the floor and they began to throw the ball to me. I proceeded to start making lay ups. Those were the days when girls played half court basketball. Either you played offense or defense. That meant you played on either side of the court. You did not run up and down the full court, something which developed in girls basketball in recent years. The coach watched helplessly as I gracefully glided across the floor, effortlessly laying up crip shots. It was obvious that I was superior to any of the girls who were actual members of the school's team. I guess I stood out so that one of the girls came to me and said, "Girl, you ought to be on our side." She said it with such volume of voice that everyone heard her, including the coach. But the coach simply sat there on the bench, never saying a word.

I decided I would make another effort to get her permission to play on the team. I decided, however, to take a little different approach. This time, I thought, I would apply a little pressure. I went to the coach's office early the next morning, while she was fresh and not besieged by the problems of the day. Once I was in her office, I said to her, "Coach, I want to be on the basketball team!" She looked at me as if to say, "I really don't believe you are back in here asking me to be on my basketball team." Her response was not that but, "I really don't have. . . " I did not allow her to complete her sentence. I said, "Well," I said, ". . .by the time I come back, I'm going to bring Ms. Maxine Smith with me. Do you know her? She's the Executive Secretary of the NAACP here in Memphis. She's my aunt's best friend. I'm going to bring her out here so she can talk to you about finding me a suit." I whirled and walked out the door, never looking back. I deliberately designed a demeanor of purpose as I exited her office. I walked down the hall and proceeded down the stairs. Before I reached the bottom of the stairs, I heard her voice with its slow southern drawl calling out to me, "Shirley, come on back up here. Let me see if I can find you something to put on to play in." I don't know if what the coach saw of me on the basketball court the previous afternoon or my threat to bring back Ms. Maxine Smith of the NAACP was the catalyst which caused her to change her mind, I do know she changed her mind about finding me a suit. She could have wanted me to help her team win some games or she could have wanted to be delivered from an encounter with the NAACP and the ensuing wrath that would come. Whichever, she proceeded to find me a suit to join the basketball team, a task that was not very difficult because I was very skinny, about size 6 or 7, and it would not be hard to find a suit for me.

I practiced hard with the team and worked myself into a position where I got to play quite frequently. However, I was only allowed to play in Memphis, on campus. I was never allowed to travel when the team went out of the city. The coach did not think white people in the South were ready for a Black player on a white team. So, I did not travel — at least for a while. I suppose it was best for the time being, there were riots going on all over the South. My presence could have caused some uneasiness in some places we had to play outside of Memphis. So, the first year, I played only in Memphis.

During the next year, I was permitted to travel with the team to Union City. That was some kind of experience. I had to ride in the car with the coach. All the white girls had their own cars. It was not unusual for white girls to have their own automobile in those days. Negroes did not have that kind of luxury. I did not have money to buy my own car. Further, in those days, schools and universities did not have money to buy a bus to carry kids. So, automobiles provided the transportation for sports teams such as ours.

When we got to Union City, I was slapped in the face with blatant racism once again. I had not gone to the locker room with the rest of the team. Something had delayed me. Finally, I began to make my way to the locker room where the other members of the team had gathered. I came down the steps and overheard the white girls talking vigorously about "Niggers." The more I descended down the steps leading to the locker room, the louder their voices became and the more I could discern what they were saying. "Did you see that Nigger. . . ." They went on and on and on. I stood in the stairway listening.

The girls had taken a ride in their automobiles about the downtown section of Union City. Once at the school, dressing for the game in the gymnasium, they compared notes on what they had seen in the center of the city. Apparently, they had seen Negroes hanging around the town square, as you often see in these small cities.

When I had heard enough and could stand it no longer, I proceeded to walk into the locker room. The girls did not see me because they were all huddled in the center of the room. They were just talking, not paying attention to anything happening around them. Finally, I coughed, just to let them know I was in the room. they looked around and saw me standing there. They were startled and stunned. They sat momentarily frozen, not able to say anything. After what seemed an eternal moment, they all came toward me, hands limp, making half-hearted gestures to show their sorrow, making feeble efforts to seek forgiveness. As they encircled me, looking at me, examining me to see if they might find an open wound oozing fresh blood from the verbal lacerations they had inflicted upon me, they all spoke in unison and poignantly vocalized their apology in concert, "We're sorry! We're sorry. We did not intend for you to hear that!" That is all they said. It was not that they did not mean what they said, they simply did not mean for me to hear what they said. I was so angry. I was too angry to say anything. I was really angry, because they did not treat me that way, or talk to me or about me, as far as I knew, like they had talked about the Negroes they had seen in Union City that day. I was surprised to hear this kind of language coming out of their mouths. I was crushed. To think I played basketball with people who talked about my people as they did, calling us "Niggers," did not make me feel very good toward them.

In that locker room, however, I could hear the voice of my grandmother saying to me, "Finish school, be somebody, love God always, put Him first and your blessings will be added to you." I heard my Aunt Mable urging me, coaxing me, "You can't let anything get you down. You have got to finish! You have got to finish!" I shrugged off the insulting conversation I had just heard and prepared to get dressed to go onto the gym floor for the basketball game we came to play.

Union City is not very far from Memphis. The people there kept up with what went on in Memphis. That included what happened at Memphis State University and her girl's basketball team. They had heard about me, the first Black woman to play basketball for Memphis State. The curious and the cautious came to see me, to see if what they had read were true. The racist and the righteous came to observe the first Black woman to play basketball for Memphis State. It was an oddity for this to occur in Union City. So, the people filled the gymnasium that night.

The coach lined up the players for their entrance into the crowded gymnasium. It was not surprising when I was placed at the very last of the line. She had always thought there might be a problem with white people not accepting me at games played outside of Memphis. This being my first such game, I suppose she was extra cautious. So, here I was. The team's only Black, still at the end of the line as we always had been throughout our existence in America. But at least, I was now on the team, even though at the end of the line. One day, I believed I would be at the head of the line in addition to being on the team.

When we started to trot out into the gymnasium, the crowd cheered as each of the white players went onto the floor. When I went onto the floor, everyone stood up in their bleacher seat and just shouted. They gave me a standing ovation. They cheered with enthusiasm. It seemed as though the people in Union City had defied the coach's expectations. She thought there would be trouble. But she looked at the crowd's reaction to my appearance and was amazed.

Being the only Black on the team created a serious problem for the coach and other team authorities. Had the keepers of society, such as coach Roane and others like her left race relations to the people, there would have been far fewer problems. The white girls on the team warmed up to me much sooner and far better than the older keepers of society, who had persuaded themselves that they knew what was better for everyone.

Because of this prevailing attitude of those who had appointed themselves to keep society as separate as possible, I had another humiliating experience when our team went to Chicago. Memphis State was to go to Chicago for a health and physical education convention. Our team was to go. I wanted to go because it was being held in Chicago. Whiletalking among members of the basketball team, I told them if we went, all of us could stay in my aunt's home in Chicago. She had a house large enough for everyone. She had three bedrooms, a dining room, and a large basement. Some of the team members could sleep on the floor. But when I approached the coach to ask permission to be included for the trip, she said no. She actually gave the reason, with her deep southern drawl, "It won't look right, one Black riding in the car with so many white people. It won't look right."

I insisted that I wanted to go. She persisted in her refusal. I went to the dean of the school and asked for permission to go to the convention. I gave the reasons for wanting to go, one of which was that I was from Chicago, was born there, had a father there. The dean gave me permission. So, I called my father and told him about the convention and that I wanted to come. He arranged to send me the money for a train ticket. Knowing their desire for me not to make the trip, I did not say anything to the coach or any of the players, or anyone else, because it was clear they did not want me to go.

I received the money from my father. I bought my train ticket. When it was time to go, I simply boarded the train for the ride to Chicago. When I arrived at Chicago, I went to where the meeting was held and made a special effort not to come in contact with them. Whenever I saw any of the team members, I walked on the other side of the street or corridor in the building where the meeting was held. I thought, "If they did not want to be bothered with me, I did not want to be bothered with them." I simply went to the classes and seminars scheduled for the convention.

Toward the end of the convention, I was walking down the corridor. I saw some of the team members from Memphis sitting to the side. I did not look at them or gesture to them as though I saw them. I kept walking. As I walked past them, I came upon some of my former classmates at Wilson Junior College. They were white, all males. We had developed a cordial relationship while I was in school in Chicago. When they saw me, the moment suddenly exploded with excitement. The corridor erupted into loud cheery chatter. My white classmates, recognizing me for who I was, rushed to me. We spent a great deal of time there in the center of the corridor reacquainting ourselves with each other. At first, my white team members from Memphis State thought the whites from Chicago were running to them. But no, they went right past them to me. They rushed right past them and grabbed me and hugged me. "Shirley, Shirley," they said, hugging me and looking at me intently with glee and gladness etched laughingly across their faces. "We're so glad to see you. Where were you? Where have you been? How come you are not in school?" They did not know I had gone south to go to school at Memphis State. As we engaged in volumes of cheery chatter, I happened to glance out of the corner of my eye to see the Memphis team members looking on in shock. Their mouths were open, their lower chin dropped in wide wonder. I never said anything to them.

When I returned to Memphis, I discovered the rumor mill running with full force. Some of the members of the basketball team came rushing to me saying, "Girl, I did not know you had white boyfriends?" I said, "What? Where did you get that from." They said, "Oh, everybody said they saw you in Chicago with your white boyfriends." They talked and they talked. I said, "I'm from Chicago. I was born in Chicago. I have plenty of people in Chicago and I have friends there." But, they tried to make a big deal out of that incident. The satisfaction I received from that experience was that the white members of my basketball team saw that I had more friends than those in Memphis. They thought I knew no one except themselves.

Toward the end of my senior year at Memphis State, I experienced another episode which characterized the racism I faced at the school. Many of the teachers in health and physical education liked me. It got to the place that when they wanted to take a break, go on an errand, or whatever the case that would take them from their class for a while, they looked for me to take over the class. I gladly did so. It happened that during those class sessions, we divided the class and made up two basketball teams to compete against each other. This eventually became an intramural situation consisting of several teams.

I chose a team consisting of the one other Black, Anita Malone, who was in the class and three whites as well as myself. We jelled as a tremendous team. In fact, we got to the place where no one could beat us. We beat up on everyone we played. We got so good that we were on the way to winning the championship in this intramural play.

I suppose some of the whites on the other teams got jealous of how good we were. They collaborated with each other to do something about our team. The way they chose to do whatever they could to destabilize us was to intimidate the three whites on the team. They planned to jump on them. One day, they cornered the three white girls in the locker room in the lower part of the gym. I was walking down the steps when I came upon them. These feminine hooligans had cornered my three girls in the locker room, and threatened them with baseball bats. I suppose they were getting ready to beat the living daylights out of them for playing with my team and beating every team we played.

Someone had left one of the bats laying on the locker room floor. That was a mistake they made. I picked up the bat and said, "If you touch them, I'll bust open the head of each of you." I really was not going to do what I said, but I acted like I was. The girls who had my girls cornered were scared to death. They dropped their bats and scattered like roaches scurrying into a dark corner when a light is turned on at night. We went on to win the championship.

My Memphis State experience was bittersweet to say the least. I had the privilege of being one of the first Blacks to attend at that time and indeed was the first to integrate the health and physical education department. But the pain endured was inexplicable. Had I not that experience, however, I do not know if there would have been an adequate measurement of what I could endure and what I could accomplish. An experience of a lesser kind, could not have proven that. As it happened, I learned how to deal with rejection and respond with fortitude and faith to over come it. I learned how to face discrimination and keep my head when all about me were losing theirs and never allow my dignity to be lowered. Really, the experience at Memphis State prepared me for what was to come later on.

What really propelled me through my Memphis State experience was the ever-present and strong support I received from my church and family. The closeness, love, concern, inspiration, and spiritual reinforcement I got from church and family were invaluable to that experience. Knowing I had the support of Aunt Mable in particular, and the rest of my family in general, was all I needed to continue on. Had I not the inner strength to fight the battles from a faith perspective, I would have lost terribly. As it happened, believing in my heart that The Lord could see me through the most trying times at Memphis State, I was able to make it. I got this spiritual strength from my church relationship. I have thanked God everyday of my life for my church.

CHAPTER XI

GRADUATING FROM MEMPHIS STATE UNIVERSITY

> Let none imagine that, because people are ignorant
> and lowly, their moral and spiritual leaders do not
> require all discipline, learning, culture and practical
> wisdom that completest education can afford. The
> more ignorant the led, the more skilful and sagacious
> should the leader be. If the blind lead the blind, will
> not both fall into the ditch?
>
> *Out of the House of Bondage*
> Kelly Miller
> 1914

Graduating from Memphis State University was one of the high points of my life. Graduation reflected the fact that I had the intellectual ability to compete with students of the other race. It also reflected the fact that I had the perseverance, discipline, and determination to complete the city's largest school, one which had only been integrated a year or two prior to my coming.

But, graduating from this school was not easy. I was taken through any number of difficult places by both students and faculty members. It appeared that some of my instructors did not want me to make it through their classes, let alone excel in them. I had an experience which demonstrated this very fact. I had an instructor who consistently gave white students "A's" but consistently gave me "C's". Obviously, she was racially prejudiced and favored the white students in the class.

I knew my lessons. Over the years, I had learned to work hard, to study hard, and to get my assignments. My grandmother instilled that in me. My Aunt Mable picked up where my grandmother left off and drove me toward excellence. I knew my work. I had it in my head. I had developed the philosophy that if you got it in your head, no one could take it from you. I strove hard to get my lessons in my head. So, I could not understand why, in this particular class, all the white students made top grades and the best I could do was a "C".

I went to the teacher and asked questions about my work. I said,

"What is wrong with my report? Show me what is wrong with my report and I will correct it. You know, I cannot make a 'C'. I am doing the best I can." Her rejoinder was, "That is all I think you deserve." I said to her, "No, Ma'am! You know I deserve better. Give me another opportunity!" I raised so much of a raucous that she said, "Okay, okay, alright, alright!" I suppose she conceded because she knew by now the whole class was looking at the two of us.

But to show how racist she was, I took a report from one of my white classmates, one which the teacher had given an "A", and rewrote it. I wrote the report verbatim, only changing the name and other particulars that would make it uniquely mine. I turned it in to the teacher, waiting to see what kind of grade she would give. When I got the report back from her, it still had a "C" on it. There was no comment, only a big "C".

I took my report to the head of the department and showed it to her. I told her that "This is so and so's report — calling the student's name as I spoke with the professor — I just copied off of her." I showed her the report I had actually written so she could compare it with the one I had copied. She said, "You mean this is what you got, a "C"? The head of the department went to talk with the teacher of the class. When she returned, the grade had been changed to a "B".

Had I not had a good educational foundation, which I received at Hamilton High School in Memphis and Wilson Junior College in Chicago, I would have folded under the racial pressure which I faced each day from my teachers. As it stood, however, I had adopted the philosophy that if I got it in my mind, no one could take it from me. With that philosophy, I drove myself to comprehend the most difficult material. I knew I could get it, whatever it was, I could comprehend it. I knew that if I got it in my head, no matter what kind of teacher I had, eventually I would pass the class and right would prevail.

These were the kinds of subtleties I had to cope with all along my academic journey at Memphis State. Instructors had little gimmicks and tricks they'd play on you to see if you could take the pressure. There was a prevailing attitude that Negroes could not learn anyway. Their little tricks and gimmicks were only designed to reinforce what they had already concluded about us. But, that is the way of prejudice.

In the area of health and physical education, it is almost expected that you emerge from your college experience as a teacher in some school, whether public or private. My last year at Memphis State saw me engage in student teaching, which was a necessary requirement for graduation. But it was student teaching which almost turned me against the field of teaching and away from it altogether.

I had some bad experiences as a student teacher. I made an "A" in my grade in the course as a student teacher, but the experience almost struck teaching from my list of employment possibilities. I was a tiny person physically. The children in the school where I was assigned were large, loud, and boisterous. They were so bad. If you told them to keep quiet, they would get quiet for a moment, only to break out afresh shortly after you had given the command. The children were negligent in their work. They seemed not to care about getting their lessons and neatly turning in their assignments to me. The classroom was so exhausting to me that each day I went home, I simply fell out on the bed and could hardly get up. When time came for me to go to school the next day, it seemed as though I could hardly put one foot before the other to go in that direction. I hated to go to school to face those tyrants, the students. So, I decided I did not want to be a teacher. I would do anything, but I would not teach.

Toward the end of my final year, some of the teachers of my department, all of whom were white, began to raise the possibility of me going to graduate school to work toward the Masters Degree. In fact, these instructors got together and went to the head of the department, the Woman's Athletic Director, and asked that she put me on the list for the graduate school program for Master's work. That must have been a "no, no" for them. In the course of events, those teachers were relieved of their duties because of their actions. At least, they did not return to the faculty the following year.

Finally, graduation day was approaching. January of 1967 came blasting in upon me like a blustery March wind. After many ups and downs, many changes and chances, it was time for me to prepare to march and receive my bachelors degree. For the administration and faculty at Memphis State, it was just another year when they went through the routine of graduating a class of students. But this was a hallmark occasion for me. This was a high watermark for Shirley Yvonne McCray. No one of my family had ever graduated from college. I had gone as far as two years at Wilson Junior College in Chicago, but I had not gotten as far as completion of a four year school of higher education. None of my family, either on my father's side or my mother's side, had accomplished this fete. I was standing on the perimeter of promise, preparing to enter the arena of achievement, getting ready to cross the finish line of a long race where a garland of grace and glory awaited.

Excitement ruled the day on campus. Each day was crammed with activities aimed at the day of graduation in January of 1967. We busied ourselves getting sized for our marching gowns and caps. Many

Shirley Yvonne McCray graduating from Memphis State University

trips were made to the administrative office to assure that all bills were current and paid in full. We anxiously checked to be sure our names were on the necessary lists of graduates.

Out in the community, excitement reigned as well. Especially at St. Jude and the home of Aunt Mable Dean Purnell, there was excitement over my imminent graduation. I felt extremely good about myself and my accomplishment. I busied myself preparing invitations for all the members of St. Jude and my immediate family. I wanted them all to be present when I received that degree in my hands.

Finally, the day came. It was one of the highest times in my life. My grandmother was not there, but her spirit was. I could feel her presence in her words, "Finish school, be somebody, love God always, put Him first and your blessings will be added to you." My aunt Mable Dean Purnell was there. She would not have missed my graduation for anything. She had done so much to make it possible for me to reach this epochal moment in my life. Aunt Mable would not allow me to work at all while going to school. Even when I began at Memphis State, I continued to work at Bruce's Box Factory, making three hundred and sometimes four hundred dollars a week. She would not allow me to give her any money. She wanted me to take all I earned and put it toward my schooling. She finally conceded to take sixty five dollars a week. But then, she turned around and went to town and bought clothes for me with the money. She simply was not going to allow me to do anything for her. She saw herself as an extension of her sister, Clara Dean McCray, my grandmother. As such, she knew my grandmother would want me to finish school at all cost.

My pastor, Reverend J. S. White, was present at my graduation. A large number of the members was present as well. The ceremony was long and drawn out. But, everything they did meant so much to me. My professors were in the entourage of faculty and administrative staff. Every teacher in the Health and Physical Education Department came

74

to see me graduate. There was an irony about their presence. They referred to me as "That smart Nigger from Chicago." They remembered me as the one who volunteered for everything they had going. They were proud that I had graduated; but also, I guess they were tired of me and were glad to see me go.

Following the ceremony, everyone, family and friends, made a great deal out of my graduation gown. Everybody wanted to take pictures with me. The afternoon was spent posing and positioning myself to be with first this one and then the other one. Aunt Mable was dressed in her finest. Her hair was fixed and fashioned unlike any time I had seen her before. We posed and took pictures together. This was the highlight of both our lives. She had seen her sister's pride and joy accom-plish a long sought goal and she had seen the fruit of her labors as well. My graduation from Memphis State University made us all want to shout hallelujah.

CHAPTER XII

INTRODUCTION TO MY CAREER IN TEACHING

Seest thou a man diligent in his business? He shall stand before kings; he shall not stand before mean men.

Proverbs 22:29

After graduation, I found myself at a loss for something to do. I did not want to get a job teaching. The experience I had in the classroom during my stint as a student teacher soured me on that profession. So, I sat around Aunt Mable's house doing nothing.

Because I had persuaded myself that I did not like children, I decided to join the United States Air Force. I signed up with the recruiter and proceeded to wait to go to Nashville to take the oath and be inducted to full time service.

While I was waiting, Aunt Mable insisted that I find some kind of job. She insisted that I could not sit around the house, I had to get a job. So, I applied for a position with the school board as a substitute teacher. I was not very particular about working in education as a teacher; but by this time, I decided that something was better than nothing.

I was fortunate to start subbing right away. There were two main high schools, Carver and Melrose, from which I could choose. These were two of the largest, predominantly Black, high schools in Memphis. Of the two, however, Carver was the worst. That school was almost under the control of gangs. They called themselves The Invaders. But, when I say gangs, I do not mean to say they were notorious in that they killed anyone and committed physical violence on people. These were robin hood type gangs. These young boys turned over cookie trucks and passed out cookies to everyone in the neighborhood. They did really silly stuff. Because of what seemed to be a great challenge, I chose Carver. I saw that school as my calling. It came to me as clear as crystal.

I taught a male instructor's class which had all boys. This man was a floating teacher. He went around to different rooms and students met him in the room. So, when I substituted for this man, I virtually did the same thing he did. I went from class to class, from the first period to the last period of the day. I noticed, however, that my class got larger and larger from day to day as we went along. I did not realize that the swollen nature of the class was due to me and the manner in which I was teaching. I was literally preaching.

By the time I had gone from class to class, from one period to the next period, at the end of the day, my classes were extraordinarily large. All I was doing was preaching and teaching. I was talking about life and what was expected of you out in the world. I was imparting to the students, all males, what they would be expected to do once they got out into the world. I was talking about respect. If you respected people, people would respect you. At one point, they called me "Preacher McCray" because I was just preaching.

What was taking place in those classrooms was a literal reproduction of what had been done in our home at Cummings and Parkway and at St. Jude Baptist Church. I was teaching and talking about life, what to expect in life, and how you should carry yourself in life. Those were the things I was taught. I was driven to teach these young boys the same things I had been taught.

The youngsters seemed to be completely fascinated with what I was saying. It may have been that they were completely fascinated with the fact that it was a skinny Black woman teacher talking to them. I weighed no more than a hundred pounds at the time.

When I got toward the sixth period at the close of the day, I had young men all around the wall in my classroom. They were not disorderly or noisy, they were just sitting or standing there looking at me and listening to me spin out my theories and philosophies about life. About the close of the day, the principal came to my room. He said, "Ms. McCray, do you have your roll? Have you been calling your roll?" I said, "Yes sir!. My class is full." I really did not know what I was saying. I did not know that the young men were not suppose to be in my classroom. They had just been following me around all day from class to class, listening to me talk about life. I continued, "I thought everybody was suppose to be here." By that time, he said, "Let me get my strap, these folk are not suppose to be here!" When he said that, a mighty roar rose up in the room. It was the thunder of students tearing out of the room to go back to wherever they were suppose to be. They almost tore down the door getting out of that room.

But, I began to raise a question with myself. What was going on here? Undoubtedly, I must have been about something here. Evidently, I thought, this is what I must be cut out to do in life. If I could hold these young men's attention like that throughout the day, I could begin to make a change in the way they think and the way they behave. If I could control their mind, I could control the child. The young men were listening to me in those classrooms. I then concluded, "This is it!!!. This is my calling!!! Teaching children!!!"

On August the 16th of 1967, I went down to the school board and said to them, "I want to teach!" The school board had already been calling me about teaching because I had been recommended by Memphis State to be a teacher. But I had refused to respond to the calls and go down to the school board and sign up. I did not want to become a teacher. But, when I walked into that office, all the administrative staff were happy to see me. They all said, "Come on in, we are going to find you a school." That was about 8:00 o'clock in the morning. By 10:00 o'clock, later in the morning, I had been assigned to a school.

All this was the fulfillment of the words of my grandmother, Clara McCray. She said, "Finish school, be somebody, love God always, put Him first and your blessings will be added to you." Getting established in a teaching career and getting an assignment to a school was indeed God's blessing. I could not see my blessing because it was clouded over by what I wanted to do myself. I wanted to join the Air Force, not thinking that it had to be God who directed my path. My blessing was discovering that I was to be a blessing to young men, who, when I started talking about life and how to live it in God and all that, simply soaked it up like a sponge soaking up water. Those young boys were hungry for what I had to offer.

Fortunately, I had not taken the oath to join the Air Force. So, I really was not obligated, legally, to go to the military. Because I had gotten clear vision from God as to what I was to do in life, I simply dodged the recruiter who signed me up for the Air Force. My family was furious with me anyway; thus, they were happy, especially my Aunt Mable, that I was going into the teaching profession.

My teaching career in Memphis began at Riverview Junior High School. This school was located on the south side of town on Majuba Street. Initially, the school consisted of portable rooms. This was the construction of the school until they built the permanent structure. Each teacher had a portable room in which they taught their class.

Once again, the community gang, the Invaders, came into play in my career as a teacher. They were not involved in my life or the life of the school in any violent way, they really were more like protectors of the neighborhood. For example, they would not allow anyone or anything to touch my portable classroom. If there were acts of violence planned to take place in the community, like had some other gang which might have really been notorious and violence prone planned to do some damage in the neighborhood, this gang saw to it that they did not bother me or whatever was mine. In fact, they made it a point to encircle my portable classroom and my automobile. They would say, tell everyone, "This is Ms. McCray's car, don't touch it!"

It came to me that this gang did involve itself in acts which resulted in damage to peoples' property. For example, they cut people's tires in the neighborhood, or put paint on some cars. But, they never bothered mine. They stood by my car and protected it. Members of the gang protected me by night and day. On one occasion, I had walked out of my house and left the front door open; either that or a strong wind blew the door open. One of the gang members, some even called them thugs, passed by my house and saw it. He got on the phone and called my school and asked for me. When the principal called me to the phone, I remarked that no one called me at school except my aunt. When I went to the phone, it was the little boy whom I knew. He called himself Johnny. He said, "Ms. McCray, I was passing your house and saw the front door was open." I said "It is?" He said, "Yes." I said, "Will you go in there and check and see if everything is alright?" He said, "I have done that already. Everything is fine and it will be until you get home. You don't need to hurry home, we gonna watch it till you get home." When I got home, it was as the young fellow said, everything was alright. Those young men saw to it that I was well taken care of.

I became fascinated with teaching when I began at Riverview. I taught health, physical education, and science. It was at Riverview Junior High School that I really began my coaching career. I began to develop all kinds of programs for the kids at school. I had gymnastic teams. I organized track and volleyball teams for girls. There were no organized basketball teams for girls in those days. But, I did organize a girl's basketball team which played in intramural tournaments, often playing against teachers. In all of this extracurricular activity, I was not getting extra pay. I was doing it because of my love for the kids. It was obvious that a deeper interest for children lay in my bosom other than teaching them how to play sports. I wanted to prepare them for life and all its opportunities. This came before me in bold relief when I started teaching at Riverview. I was practicing my track team when I noticed a little girl, Linda Lanton, standing on the side of the school building watching me practice my girls. Each day, I noticed her standing there. She was a little sixth grader. One day, she came to me and said, "I want to be on your track team." I said, "Baby, you got to be in the seventh grade to be on this track team." She said, "I think I can run with your children." I said, "Sure, come on." From that day on, that young lady became a member of my track team and a close friend of mine. When she came to Riverview as a student the next year, she was a straight "A" student. In each grade, she was very smart, most of the time making straight "A's". She was a good track runner. She broke all kinds of records running track.

I had never met her mother, until later. She would never be at home when I took the youngster home from track practice. The little girl usually made it on her own.

One day I was looking through an educational magazine and saw an advertisement concerning a prep program for bright children. It said you could send information concerning a student and there was a chance that student could get a scholarship, if he or she were smart enough. I sent off information concerning Linda to New Hampshire, the address in the advertisement. I informed them how smart the girl was, how she could run track, how good she was, and the kind of personality she had. In response to the information I sent them, they sent a scholarship and plane ticket for her to come to New Hampshire. I told her mother about the good fortune. The mother had a fit. She didn't want her to go. She wanted her to stay and help with the younger children. The little girl cried and cried.

I did not know what to do about the situation. I talked with the guidance counselor about the matter. She said, "I am with you." We both bought the child some clothes, got her set and took her to the airport and put her on a plane. This young girl graduated from that prep school, Phillips Exeter Academy, *Cum Laude*. Eventually, she got a scholarship at Cornell University and graduated second in her class. She was the second to graduate from Cornell in architectural engineering since 1891. She went on to Chicago, Illinois and earned a masters of business administration from the University of Illinois. She then went to work on Wall Street in New York City. She was the first Black to work on Wall Street. Following that, she worked for Sachs, Goldman Sachs. She later went back to school and got a law degree. Now, she buys and sells companies for Motorola. She travels all over the world buying and selling companies for Motorola. She did all this because I motivated her.

Sometimes, parents do not know or understand how to motivate and inspire their children. Linda, however, through her success, has been able to motivate and assist at least three of her brothers and sisters through college.

At Riverview, I was successful in organizing girls' teams in almost every sport. We had basketball, volleyball, track, gymnastics and the like. All this was for girls. I guess I was too successful for my own good at Riverview. For whatever reason, I suddenly received a special delivery from the Board of Education stating that I was being transferred.

Riverview Athletic Association • Riverview Junior High School

The transfer was to an all-white school, Kingsbury High School.

My transfer to Kingsbury High School was in 1970. I stayed there three years, 1970 to 1973. My transfer was the white administration-run school system's way of integrating schools. They used a universal plan which was employed across the country to integrate schools. They took the best teachers, Black and/or white, and placed them in the schools in white communities. With whatever remained, the worst of the teaching corps, whether Black or white, they sent to inner city schools. That meant that inner city students were pushed further down than other parts of the community. It meant that we would lose control of our children, and we would have to work doubly hard to maintain whatever semblance of control we could. We were unaware of it at the time but we were being placed in a sinking ship and nobody but God could save us then and nobody but God can save us now.

My teaching experience at Kingsbury High School was revealing. I learned much about the thinking of white people about Negroes. In my class in health and physical education, one white child told me that white people told her that all Black people had peanut brains. That meant Black people could not think. The child wanted to know if that were true. My response was to begin discussing the different charac-teristics about whites and Blacks and the categories we place each other in. I drew these categories on the chalk board. We then began

82

to talk about the categories. Into the conversation, I began to point out how silly it was for one race to think of the other as we do. I knew the youngsters ran home to tell their parents what was discussed in the class, but, it was in those kinds of conversations and class discussions that I gained the respect of the whites at Kingsbury. All the students, in this school which was predominantly white, referred to me as "Yes Ma'am" and "No Ma'am." All the time I was there, only a very few of them would say to me, "yea" or "naugh." They always addressed me in a respectful manner.

I found racism at Kingsbury just as I had at Memphis State University. It was there at the very top, among the teachers and administration. None of the teachers talked with me, except those who worked with me in the gym. I was the only Black on the faculty. My only significant relationship was with the students I taught.

I had one gym teacher with whom I developed a good relationship. He was a coach and taught a boys class in volleyball. We were very close. One day he approached me with a request to teach his boys class while he taught the girls course in golf. I said, "Sure."

I proceeded to teach these high school boys volleyball. They already knew the game quite well. I had them sitting on the floor while I showed them some techniques in the volleyball serve. The young fellows had me cracking up while I was trying to teach them the serve. They continued to act up, cracking jokes, and acting crazy. The guys were sitting on the floor, some with their legs crossed and others with their legs open. I was really into teaching them about the serve, when all of a sudden the boys broke out in roaring laughter. I stopped what I was doing and looked

Shirley McCray proudly poses as a coach at Kingsbury.

at them with the ball tucked under my arm. I said to them, "What is so funny? All you guys do is sit around here and giggle, like a bunch of girls." I continued with a bit more vigor, not really knowing what was getting ready to come out of my mouth, "You act like a bunch of nuts!" Sitting there on the gym floor, they all turned and looked at one then the other. Then they looked down. Then, they busted out laughing uncontrollably. I then realized what I had said. I had said, "You are acting like a bunch of nuts!" By looking down at themselves, they were saying they were a bunch of nuts. They just did not open their mouths to say so. Wrung tight with laughter, they all turned red. Realizing what had just happened, I turned and walked out of the class. When I saw the teacher, I said, "You've got a crazy class." He jokingly said, "Yes, I know. Don't you just love them?"

From the years I spent at Kingsbury High School, I developed a rapport with the students which was admirable. When I left the school, my love for them and their love for me remained. If ever I came across any of them in some public place, they acted as if I were the Queen of Sheba. They would run and grab me and hug me, saying they were glad to see me.

It was obvious that I could not remain at Kingsbury, the school was located in an all white community. They did not need me so much, surely they could get along without me. I constantly heard the call of my people in the heart of the city. To that call, I had to be faithful.

BOOK IV

CHAPTER XIII

MY COACHING GENESIS: A WOMAN BREAKING INTO A MAN'S WORLD

"It's a man's world—"
James Brown

The beginning of my coaching career actually came with my decision to leave Kingsbury High School and go back to an inner city school which was predominantly Black. I had done a little coaching here and there prior to this, but none of any significance. My involvement was more teaching than coaching. I taught some volleyball, track, basketball, and the like at Riverview Junior High and Kingsbury High School. But, actually coaching a team in league competition came with my move to the inner city.

At Kingsbury, I had a *deja vu* feeling which increasingly thrust me back into the mood I felt while in Chicago. There was this haunting feeling that I was moving in circles, not getting very much done in life. I was teaching white children whose parents owned businesses, had money, and means to guarantee them success without much effort. I was trying to encourage them to learn, go to college, and all the good things I knew and had been taught. They were responding to me with, "Ms. McCray, my dad owns so and so." Or, they'd say, "I'm going to get this job or that job." They'd even tell me, "I don't need to go to college." I felt helpless and hopeless. Here I was trying to tell them of the importance of getting an education, the importance of finishing high school, the importance of their livelihood. They were responding to my passion and painful encouragement with a nonchalant dismissal of the effort. Thanks but no thanks was what they were saying to me. I felt I was not accomplishing what I should as a teacher. It was not fulfilling at all to be at Kingsbury. I decided I needed to leave.

I arranged a meeting with the officials at the Board of Education. At that meeting, I requested reassignment to a school in the inner city which had a predominantly Black student population. There was no equivocation on their part. They immediately assigned me to Chickasaw Junior High School. This school was located on Westmont in Memphis.

The school board had recently restored girls basketball back into the

Coach McCray and gymnastic team,
Chickasaw Junior High School

athletic program of the system. Just as importantly, the position I was to assume was with pay. This would be the first time I would receive pay for my work in athletics in the school system. Previously, all I did with kids, the work I did at Riverview and Kingsbury, was without pay. Picking up children, carrying them home after practice and meets or games, was all done at my expense. Whatever I did, I did it on my teacher's salary. But now, my work at Chickasaw with the girls basketball team would be with pay. I was excited about that. Everyone can use more money.

I went to Chickasaw to coach the girls' basketball team — I thought. When I got there, things turned out to be different. Quite naturally, going into a new situation, you do so as the lowest person on the seniority totem pole. This was the case with me and it proved to be the undoing of my brief assignment as coach of the girls' basketball team. Coach Chapman was already at Chickasaw when I arrived. He was one of the assistant coaches of the seventh and eighth grade boys football team, but he was not doing very well with them. He was not winning. He was dissatisfied with his progress. So, he thought he could do better with the girls basketball team. He moved quickly to take advantage of his seniority and claimed the coaching position that was available with the girls' basketball team. That left me without a position of coaching the girls basketball team, the job I went to Chickasaw to assume. Painfully, I came into the awareness that there was nothing I could do about it.

The male coaches supported Coach Chapman's move. In fact, they all thought it was funny, namely, that he should block me from coaching the girls basketball team. That left me with the alternative of not coaching at all or doing what they thought was the undoable, *viz.,* coaching an all-boys football team. When I registered a complaint about him stepping in front of me and taking the position of coach of the girls basketball team, pejoratively, Coach Chapman said to me, "If you want to coach so bad, go on out there and coach those old hard headed boys. I'm tired of them anyway. I ain't winning."

I did not know anything about football. All I knew was somebody kicked the ball, someone else threw it, and then another caught the ball. That is all I knew. More than that, I did not know anything about coaching an all-boys football team. I had not coached an all-boys anything heretofore. This was new territory for my thinking.

But, I decided to accept his dare. I thought, "You haven't said anything." I will take on this challenge, like I have taken on other challenges in my life. And, I will master the challenge." So, I got myself ready mentally, as best I could, to go before the team the next day.

The football team for which I was to assume coaching responsibilities was made up of boys in the seventh and eighth grades. This was the basic team, where the players learned the basics of the game of football. They learned fundamental plays, how to handle their position, and there were a few games during the season. After playing in this capacity for the seventh and eighth grades, these boys automatically moved up to the ninth grade team utilizing the knowledge and skills of the game which they acquired the previous two years. In other words, I became responsible for preparing the young players for the varsity team in the 9th grade. How well I prepared them in the 7th and 8th grades determined the kind of team we would have later on. That was a great challenge and a great responsibility.

So, rather than taking the helm of the girls' basketball team at

Chickasaw Football Team and Coach McCray (top left) - 1977

Chickasaw, the next day after the dare, I went before the boys on the football team for the seventh and eighth grades. When I walked out on the field, they all were surprised to see me, a woman, as their coach. Some of the little fellows had a rather sad look on their faces. It was as if to say, "What is this woman going to do?" I was compelled to assume an air of confidence, even though I really did not know what was going on. To be honest, I did not know a tackle from a guard. I did not have one clue to what a play was. This was all new to me! I knew how to coach sports like volleyball, track, gymnastics, tennis, badminton, golf, and the like, but I did not know the game of football.

I concluded quickly that if I were to coach this team, I had to learn the game — and that I had to do quickly. To exacerbate the situation, in making the switch, Coach Chapman created a condition where he would receive a salary for coaching the girls basketball team but I would not receive pay for coaching the boys team. So, he really placed me in a situation of double jeopardy. I was at once faced with the task of coaching a boys football team, something I had never done before and at the same time I would not receive pay for my labor.

Neither incumbrance served as a deterrent. I was determined to assume the challenge of coaching these boys and developing them into a good football team. I had to learn the game, but that would not prove difficult. I had learned all the other games, I would learn this one as well.

From the time I accepted Coach Chapman's dare, I sought to learn everything I could about the game itself and all its positions. I went out and watched every football game I could. I watched football games on TV. I talked to as many coaches as possible, those who would talk with me about the game. Even the boys on the team taught me some of the particulars of the game. If I placed someone in the wrong place, if I'd say, "You come over here and play this position," they'd say, "No, coach, the guard goes there next to the center" or something on that order. It got to the place where the boys were as helpful as anyone.

In trying to become the best coach possible, I sought help from any and every source possible. When other coaches saw me or heard of me coaching my team, they would send plays through the mail. I attended conventions across the state, the University of Tennessee at Chattanooga, the University of Tennessee at Martin, as well as in Memphis at Memphis State University to glean any information I could about the game. At those conventions, coaches would write out plays and pass them to me. I was forced to sit on the front row at those conventions, because the men were so tall, big and husky that I could not see over them if I sat in the rear of the room. So, I sat on the front row in order the hear and see what was being drawn on the chalk board. These conventions were really fruitful because I developed relationships which lasted. Coaches would send me plays all the time but would not sign their name. I remember reading Bear Bryant's book *On Winning Football* and underlining his philosophy about football. I adopted his philosophy because he was one of the winningest coaches in football history, I wanted to be a winning coach.

I wanted to be a winning coach so badly that I paid my own expenses to all the conventions and coaches meetings I attended. Noticeably, I was the only Black attending those meetings, most of the time. If black male coaches were in attendance, they were few and far between. There seemed to be a prevailing attitude among them that reflected a contempt for teaching. They seemed to say, by their absence and in other ways, that they did not need to be taught what they already knew. I did not feel that way, I needed to find out all I could to become a good coach and produce a winning football team. So, it was a small thing for me to pay my own way. I discovered that Black male coaches would receive pay for attending the same meetings I attended. But I was not eligible for similar pay, because I was a woman. That kind of discrimination was not a deterrent, however, I wanted to win football games. I decided I had to do what I had to do in order to win.

The person most helpful in getting me equipped for coaching was a member of my church, St. Jude Baptist Church. He was Bro. Hosea Alexander, a deacon in our church. He was a teacher, coach, and assistant principal in the city school system, and one of the winningest football coaches there was. Even before I began to coach, he impressed me so much because he brought the players on his football team to church. He had them sit in the back of the church. Every time he had a football game, he brought his players to church. When I began to coach, I decided then that I wanted to be like him and bring my players to church. This, I thought, would go a long way in the players' personal, intellectual, moral, spiritual, as well as physical development. I wanted my approach to coaching to be of such that I sought to develop the total person.

I went to Bro. Hosea Alexander and inquired of him how I might put together plays which would produce a winning team. He sat me down and showed me how the game was played. He took out all the film he had from football games. From these, he demonstrated plays and wrote them down and showed how they were to be executed. He showed me what to look for in choosing young men to play the game. He gave me pointers on what kind of young man I should place on the line, what kind of player I should look for to put in the backfield.

Coach Alexander was excellent. He gave me all I needed to put together a winning team. In fact, I went back to the team at Chickasaw and employed all he said and we started winning football games.

But breaking into this man's world of coaching male football teams was fraught with discouraging factors all along the journey. I met discouragement all the way from the school's administration to my fellow coaches. Discrimination in pay was a potential deterrent, but I never allowed that to dampen my enthusiasm for the job. It could have had I let it. When I first went to Chickasaw Junior High School, I was not that much concerned about pay. I had been so used to not receiving pay that it did not register with me as being of serious importance. I spent my time learning the game and learning how to coach the game. The next year, however, I became concerned because I knew the male coaches were being paid but I was not. I went to the principal of Chickasaw and asked if I were going to get paid. He said to me, "No". I took it. I did not like it, but I took it. It hurt to know that the gentleman who took my job through the conveniences of seniority was being paid, but I was not because I was a woman.

The following year, it was discovered that I was the only woman football coach in the United States coaching an all male football team. The necessary research was done to authenticate this fact. The school librarian sent the information to Ebony Magazine in Chicago, Illinois and they began to write stories about me. Because of the coverage I received in Ebony Magazine and later on in Jet Magazine, the local newspapers began to cover what I was doing in the field of coaching as well.

Because of this increasing fame and improvement in my game, I went to the principal again to ask if I could get paid for coaching. He emphatically stated, "No!" And he further said to me, "If you don't like it, quit!" For him, it was as simple as that. I left his office determined not to allow pay inequity to dissuade me from coaching and shaping the lives of young men who possibly could become outstanding in society. Pay was not everything, after all, I felt The Lord would provide for me whatever financial assistance I needed. But, I must admit, had lack of pay been reason for me discontinuing my coaching, it could have done so.

If insults and prejudicial statements were reason enough for me to stop what I was doing, they would have done the dirty deed, they would have delivered the lethal blow. I had enough of them hurled at me. I was never faced with disrespect from my players. The way I trained them, disciplined them and got them in shape, the kind of positive reinforcement I gave them, almost like a mother caring for a child as well as being a good coach for them, elicited from them their highest respect. But it was the male coaches who openly demonstrated their contemptuous behavior toward me.

In one of my years at Chickasaw, a year when I had put together an unbeatable team, one of the male coaches stung me with an insult. We had beaten his team 30 to 0. I had put together a strong team that year. As we departed the playing field, all my players were happy, even exuberant. Everyone was congratulating me about the win. This particular team had not been beaten prior to this game. They really thought they were unbeatable, but we showed them a thing or two. Our win, as well as the score, was humiliating for their team. On the way off the field, the coach walked over to me and said, "Well, you did not win because you are a good coach, you won because you had some horses." It hurt my pride for him to say that, because I had worked so hard to develop my boys. He was saying I had not done anything to develop them, they had developed themselves. I knew that was not so. I said to him, "The horses had to be guided!" But before I could shrug off his first insult, he hurled another at me. He said, "You need to be at home cooking!" I saw that this man liked to hit you where it hurt. But I braced up and walked on off the field with my head high and a win tucked under my tunic. He could not take that away from me.

I took coaching seriously. I stayed up nights studying plays. I got to the place where I would not sleep at night because of my intense study of football plays. Particularly the night before a game, I got no sleep at all. I stayed up all night planning, drawing up plays, working through each one of them, making sure I had them down and the player best suited to carry them out.

At the same time I was doing all this, I was deeply involved in the life of my church. I was directing the choir at St. Jude. I worked with the young people. I was at church everyday. I went on Tuesday nights for Sunday school teachers' meeting and on Wednesday night for choir rehearsal. Some Saturdays, we'd meet at the church for choir rehearsal. When I was in charge of the youth of the church, I picked them up in my vehicle and delivered them back home as well. But all this began to take its toll on my physical being and psychic stability. I began to have blood pressure problems and was continuously physically tired. So, I was compelled to lessen some of my activities and the intensity of my involvement in both church and football.

Breaking into this man's world of coaching male athletes was not easy in any stretch of the imagination. But having found myself in the arena, I loathed the idea of trying to find a way to extricate myself from the challenge. I found myself doing all I could to prove my worth as a coach. I was like the Apostle Paul when he said, nothing ". . . shall be able to separate us from the Love of God which is in Christ Jesus our Lord." I decided to let nothing separate me from my love for coaching boys in football. If it were the price of coaching without pay, I was willing to pay that. If it were the price of pursuing consultation at my own expense, I was willing to pay that price. If it were necessary that I endure sleepless nights in order to have a well-planned and coached game the next day, I could manage that cost. If it cost me physical distress and mental anguish, I would draw heavily from the Bank of God's mercy and grace to have the revenue I needed. I wanted to be the best coach I could be in this all-man's world.

CHAPTER XIV

COACHING WITH TEARS AND A BROKEN HEART

Oh that my head were waters, and mine eyes
a fountain of tears, that I might weep day
and night for the slain of the daughter of my
people!

Jeremiah 9:1

Coaching for me was as much guts as it was glory. In fact, it was more guts than glory. Coaching was as much tears as it was toughness. I had to be tough! I had to be tough in mind, tough in spirit, and tough in the flesh. But I found it necessary to temper toughness with tenderness. Often, my toughness was constrained to yield to tears.

If there is anything I have learned from being a woman coaching all males, it is that she has the advantage of freely allowing her emotions to flow and affect the lives of the players in positive and productive ways. This is not to say that emotions are used to influence the players one way or other, it means the female coach becomes intimately involved with her players in a way male coaches do not, cannot, or will not. In other words, I was as much mother to my players as I was coach. That gave me leverage with my players that I might not have had otherwise.

When I started out, I was determined to be a good teacher. It came to me that being a good teacher is prerequisite for being a good coach. You cannot be a good coach if you are not a good teacher. It simply is not possible.

The next thing I came upon was that I had the knack for talking to children and getting them to do what I wanted them to do. Later on, I determined that if I could control the mind, I could control the child. I found that to be true. To a great extent, this is where much of the problem is. We do not control our children's thinking, we do not control their minds. But it is possible to control a child's mind. It is possible for a mother to control her child's thinking. In fact, if she begins this process from the time of conception, she will control that child for as long as that child is in the world.

This concept has much to do with my philosophy of coaching. As a mother figure, I can nurture the players and talk to them and get them to do what they need to do to be good citizens, as well as good football players. With this approach, there are four things I have tried to get over to a player, 1) the importance of physical fitness, 2) mental clarity and sturdiness, 3) being sociable, being a good sport, 4) and being spiritually molded. As a mother figure, I tried to get all this across to the players.

I literally got involved in my player's life, in the sense of those four things I try to get over to them. At school, I was their teacher, especially if they took health, physical education, or science. Thus, I assisted them in getting their lessons and passing in their grades. When it came time to practice, I was their coach. I pushed them in drills to get out of them all that was in them. When they sat down to rest, I took that opportunity to preach to them the gospel of morals, ethics, and spiritual strength. I taught them the importance of prayer. After every practice session, we closed with prayer. We prayed after every game. The players became conditioned to this ritual, so much so that if I forgot to lead them in a prayer, they leaped at the opportunity to remind me.

Once following a practice session, I was so tired that I forget to lead the team in prayer before dismissal. We had worked real hard that day. I had sent the team through running drills, blocking drills, pass plays, running plays, and a whole assortment of things which were designed to get them ready for a game. I was tired. When they completed their drills, I turned and started to walk to the gymnasium. I was unaware that I had failed to led the team in prayer. Oblivious to my omission, I proceeded to walk toward the gymnasium. I sensed that no one was walking along with me. I looked back saying, "Where is everybody?" When I looked, the players were on their knees. I was almost back at the gymnasium. I spun around and shouted to them, "Come on!" They said, "Uh Uh, Coach, you come on back, we have not had prayer." I felt very bad. Here I was teaching my team the necessity of prayer. I forgot, and they reminded me. When I collected myself, it did make me feel rather good to know that I had gotten over the lesson of the importance of prayer in the life of my football players.

When practice was concluded, after we had our prayer, I nursed their wounds and saw to it that their physical needs were taken care of. Then, I washed the players uniforms, like a good mother. I mended the tears on the uniforms. I saw to it that their playing gear was in tact and all together.

I suppose one very important way I won the loyalty and trust of my players was that I virtually became a part of their lives, and the lives of their family. I still believed that a strong family and a strong church meant so much to the development of an individual. So, I worked hard to know the kid's mother and father, if there was a father in the home. Quite often there was not a father figure in the home.

This closeness to player and family brought with it a particular emotional attachment which dug deep into the heart. Whatever affected my players affected me. I was tough in many ways, but when it came to my players, there was a kind of tenderness which could tear open my heart and drive precipitous tears from my eyes. I had noticed that male coaches did not permit themselves to get emotionally involved with their players. I always had a feeling that such would be an advantage if they would employ it.

This tumult of the spirit came upon me when I lost my first football player to death. Carl Lang was a player on my team of 1977 at Chickasaw. He had saved the day for us and won the game with the only touchdown that day. We had played the opposing team to a nothing to nothing tie. We thought the game would end that way. But just at the last of the game. Carl caught the kick deep in our territory. He took off running with the ball. He was strong. He ran past everybody and on down the sidelines and entered into the end zone untouched by anyone. We won that game and Carl ran the only touchdown of the game.

We held practice the next Monday. Everybody was filled with gleeful excitement over our win. We had not played but one game for the season and we were looking forward to having a good year. By Wednesday, Carl Lang who had run the touchdown the previous Saturday, came to me and said, "Coach McCray, my stomach is hurting so bad." I said, Oh boy, you just need to go to the bathroom." His face was contorted in such a way that I knew it was more than a simple stomach ache. He said, "Uh uh, Coach, this is another kind of hurt." I said, "Well, when you go home, you tell your mother to give you an *Alka Seltzer*." When he got home, he told his mother about his problem. Just as I had told him to tell her, she gave him an *Alka Seltzer*. He got worse. She rushed him to the emergency room of the hospital.

The doctors checked him out. After giving him a thorough going over, the doctors returned to the mother and told her that the boy would not live more than thirty days. She became hysterical. "For what, for what, what is wrong with him?" she screamed at the doctor. "He has just had a physical two or three weeks ago and he was perfect then, what is wrong now?" The doctor tried to calm her down. He said to her quietly, "You son is dying from leukemia. He will be dead in less than thirty days."

Because I was close to the family, like a mother to them all, this mother called me in complete hysteria. I could hardly tell what she was saying. She was in such a confused state of mind. I knew something terrible was wrong, so I prepared to go to the home to meet them. When I got there, they had arrived back from the hospital. The doctors had allowed the boy to return home as well. The mother was still crying. I tried to calm her and comfort her. She kept crying. Finally, she calmed down enough to tell me the news. Her son only had a short time to live. He was dying from leukemia.

The young boy, only twelve years old, spoke to us all with an authority known only to few adults. "I'm going to be okay," he said. "Don't you know, I'm alright with the Lord?" Now, here was a twelve year old boy giving his parents and superior in football lessons on how to deal with death. On his sick bed, only days away from his last breath, he demonstrated a stronger faith in God than those of us who had travelled down the road of life many years longer than he.

It was hard, though. From that time on, he would go into the hospital and come back out. His doctor was extremely careful not to allow him to get exhausted or expose himself unduly to germs which could exacerbate his situation. In all of this, I was intimately involved. His mother would call me. We would talk about her son's situation. We would pray about it over the phone. Carl would call me, we would talk and pray over the phone. I tried to comfort him by composing a musical arrangement which encouraged him to trust in the Lord, to read his Bible, and to play the songs I had arranged and given him on a tape recording. I told him that when he got discouraged to read what I gave him and play the songs. I hoped this would be effective in cheering him up. But, the more we sought to comfort him, the more he taught us how to deal with the inevitable — death. We all tried so hard to deal with the slow demise of this young fellow, but the more we looked at him, the more difficult it became.

I could hardly deal with what was unfolding before my eyes. A week or so ago, this young man was racing down the football field with the winning touchdown in his hands. And now, he was lying on a bed that would lay claim to him in death. but, he said to us all, "Don't you know, I'm alright with Jesus?" With the confidence of a veteran Christian soldier, he said to us, "Don't you realize that if I leave here today, I'm going to heaven?"

The mercy of God is great. He knew how much we could bear. Only a few merciful days passed before the time came for us to reckon with reality. We received a call from the doctor at the hospital. He said, "You need to come now. It won't be long. He is getting ready to go."

We arrived at the hospital. His parents and I arrived about the same time. We made our way through the main entrance of the hospital and onto the elevator to the floor on which he was located. When we arrived in the area, they had placed the young boy in a glass cubicle. We all were standing outside, but we could see him. When he raised up and saw me, he said, "Hey Coach!" You could hear him, for there was a window opening in the cubicle. I pitched my voice up so he could hear me, "How are you feeling?" I said inquiringly. With an unusual lightness and glee, he said, "I feel fine. I feel just fine. I don't have a hurt nowhere." I said, "That sounds good." His dad and mom looked

Carl Lang, 1961-1976

at me and I returned the glance. We all were quizzical about this comment, wondering really what was going on. How could he be feeling so fine without a pain, a hurt, if he were even now feeling the misty sprays of the Jordan River of Death? That was the question which was framed in the expression on our faces. I could see the hurt in the parents' eyes. The doctors had already told them their son was dying. They knew it was not long.

Somehow, none of us wanted to concede to the wrath of reality. We secretly were hoping against hope that some miracle would just now happen — that this young man could be snatched back from the swirling currents of the Jordan River of Death. For a while, the boy was laughing and talking. Sometimes, it seems, the dying demonstrate a surge of energy and seeming improvement in conditions before they succumb to the grasp of death. He had us doing the same. In fact, we found ourselves standing in the hospital room talking and sometimes puncturing our conversations with guarded laughter.

Suddenly, the room got dreadfully quiet. The boy looked at us through the glass cubicle and said with a strong voice, "Why is everybody so quiet? Say something, do something." When he said that, we all started laughing and talking again, our way of spreading salve over the wounds which were opening in our hearts. Then, the little fellow looked at me, then he looked at his mother. He glanced over at his father. He took a deep breath. Closed his eyes. And, he died.

Nurses and orderlies had to pull me out of the room and carry me to a nearby hospital. I hollered and cried. I hollered and cried until I could not holler and cry any more. They had to give me some kind of shot to calm me down. My heart was broken.

The ordeal of losing young Carl brought the words of the Psalmist David full force into my mind:

> *My tears have been my meat*
> *day and night.*
> Ps. 42:3a.

All I did for days, weeks, following the death of Carl, was cry. It took me weeks to get over his death. I could not go back to school. I could not teach. It was so bad that when I did attempt to resume my teaching and classroom duties, I would attempt to teach and tears would roll down my cheeks. I just could not deal with Carl's death. I had taken him, just as I had all my players, as my own son. It was like I had lost one of my children. I had put so much energy into developing him, as I would my own child. His loss drove me to endless tears and a fractured, broken heart.

These kind of heart rending episodes were sprinkled throughout my coaching career. At every school, from Riverview to Booker. T. Washington High School, I often coached through tears and a broken heart. I guess it comes naturally when you identify with those whom you lead. I had sat where these young men sat. I had lived where they lived and grown up as they had grown up. I knew the problems they faced. I simply was trying to give them the tools to work with to lift themselves above the morass of the really real situation in which they found themselves. I found myself entwined in their entire lives, their sickness and health as well, their good fortunes and fatalities as well, their life and in their death.

In taking this approach to coaching, there were cases which presented themselves everyday which elicited my tears and heartache. There was this very dark young man whom I discovered one day and asked if he would play football for me. He said he would not mind it, but was certain that his mother would not permit it. When I inquired of his mother, she informed me that he was an epileptic and it would not be good for him to play. I ask her why that was the case. She responded, "Because, I can not always be with him to give him his medicine." I told her that was not a problem, I would give him his medicine.

What I discovered, I not only had to give the young man his medicine for epilepsy, I had to be his nurse, doctor, and mother when his mother was not there. He proved to be an excellent football player. He was one of the fastest runners I ever had. But, when he was threatening a seizure, I had to be right on the spot to give him his medicine. I had to watch him closely, every minute he was in my care.

Heartbreak and tears came because of this young man as it had for others. Time wound up for Booker T. Myles, the young man. His condition grew more severe and he was lost to death at an early age. He went to Chicago to visit his father. When he got there, he told his father he was tired and wanted to lie down. He did, and went to sleep. He never woke from that sleep.

Once again, I had entangled myself in the family webbing of one of the players on my team. And, once again, I was driven to tears and my heart was broken because of his death. But, over the years of my career as a coach, this became for me a usual occurrence.

CHAPTER XV

FROM CHUMPS TO CHAMPS

The heights by great men reached and kept
Were not attained by sudden flight,
But they, while their companions slept,
Were toiling upward in the night.
The Ladder of St. Augustine
Henry Wadsworth Longfellow

When I went to Chickasaw Junior High School in 1973, I was faced with formidable opposition in every way. When I accepted the coach's dare to coach those hard headed boys, I became a "woman coach" intruding into a "man's world." Entering into a man's world of coaching football, I discovered, would be a serious hurdle to clear. To add to the difficulty, I had not coached football. I did not know the game as I did other sports. Finally, I had never coached all boys in any sport. I had an uphill journey before me, one with extremely slippery conditions to navigate.

My efforts with the Chickasaw Junior High School football team brought only negligible results at the beginning. It was like trying to make brick without straw. The first two years, we won only a couple of games out of the schedule of five games each year. The two games we won were by default, the teams did not show up for the contest. They simply did not have a team. But then, no one looked for us to win any game. We were chumps. We would never have a presence in the world of football, I was a woman trying to do a man's job. Probably, this was the intention when the coach set the dare before me. He and his comrades probably felt that after awhile I would simply throw in the towel. They assumed that they need not bother with me, with my limited knowledge and the raw materials I had to work with, I would not last long in this fiery trial. But, they did not know Shirley Yvonne McCray. I had never conditioned my mind to settle for being chumps, I had always aspired to be the best of whatever I attempted. I would do no less in this endeavor. I decided to do my best to make champs of this team.

I proceeded to use the early days with my team as a time to bond with the players, a time to share with them my philosophy about football,

101

a time to share with them my spirit and determination. I talked to them about life. I tried to show the team members that football presented situations which were similar to life. There were barriers which you had to over come in life, just as you had in football. "You must set your goals in life," I told them, "just as you have a goal in football . . . An aggressive person sets goals in life and tries to accomplish them. If you set your goals, then you try to reach them." I continued to teach them, "There are a lot of blockages in front of you, but you have to learn how to maneuver through those things in life, just as you have to do on the football field." I kept working on the theory that if I could control the mind of my players, I could coach them and get them to do the kinds of things that would get them to the winner's circle. I firmly believed this and I worked hard to get them to believe it as well.

I employed another of my penchants as a female coach, that of wielding my motherly influence. Many of the boys thought of me as they thought of their mother. This made it even easier for me. On that field, I was not only those youngsters' coach, I was their mother. I knew that. I knew that if I could translate that from home to the football field, I could control those boys. I also knew that if I could translate that motherly love into motherly authority, I could get the young men to obediently carry out their assignments on the field. I tried to utilize this to the maximum. Thus, I taught my boys to be neat and orderly in everything they did. This was my motherly instinct. I taught them how to dress, how to match colors, how to match clothes. I taught them how to arrange their knife, fork, and napkin at the dinner table. I taught them to pick up their clothes and place them in an orderly manner in their proper place. These were things male coaches simply did not think to do. But, they were things the boys realized they could use off the field, at home, in society, and later on in life when they were no longer under the influence of their coach or parent. I took advantage of such insight and made good use of it.

One of my boys took my teachings about neatness, orderliness, and cleanliness so seriously that his mother developed a love/hate attitude toward me. I saw her at an office I was visiting on business for my Aunt Mable. When I saw her, I said, "I know you!" She said, "Yes, my son was on your football team." After some small talk, she said to me, "You know what, I never said thanks to you but you did wonders for my son. When you talked to him about picking up his clothes and cleaning up after himself, girl, he's so neat now that he makes me sick." Almost apologetically, she continued on, "He said, 'Coach McCray told me how to fold my clothes.' He even began to teach me, telling me, 'You should not lay down your clothes like that, Coach McCray said you should hang up your clothes when you walk in the house.' Everything you tried to do, it was 'Coach McCray said. . . .'" She kept on talking and finally said, "I stayed mad at you for a long time. But, when I saw the end result of what it did for my child, I couldn't say anything but thank you." That was the kind of influence I cultivated with the parents as well as their sons who played on my team. It was a wonderful experience in bonding. I was able to get those boys to do almost anything I wanted them to do, to give all they could while playing the game of football.

I was peculiarly interested in the manner in which Coach Alexander controlled the moral and ethical behavior of his players. I concluded this was done through the practice of taking his players to church to worship on Sunday. I made that a requirement for all players on my team. I wanted them to see me directing the youth choir. I wanted them to see the youth of the church in action. I wanted them to see their coach in action doing something other than hollering at them on a football field. The practice of carrying them to church cultivated a mellower spirit for the players and reinforced the moral and ethical maxims I was teaching them on a daily basis.

I spent a great deal of time getting myself personally prepared to develop a winning team. The time I spent with Coach Hosea Alexander was extremely profitable. I went over the material he shared with me time and time again. I tried to master every modicum of his methods. So much of what Coach Alexander gave me I found to be quite effective in developing a top rate football team. It was because of my utilization of his theories, philosophies, and plays, that I was able to move my team from chumps to champs.

When I went to conventions to listen to the great coaches of the nation, I studied them thoroughly. Sometimes I did not sleep until I had mastered each play they gave me or mailed me following one of the conventions. This was true of Coach Bear Bryant's book which I bought at one of those meetings. His book, *Bear Bryant On Winning Football*, articulated many of the coaching philosophies I had formed on my own. When I discovered that one of the nation's winningest coaches in football held many of the same philosophies as I, I became enamored with him and blended his thinking with mine. I read his book thoroughly, from cover to cover, savoring each page and paragraph, squeezing from each syllable morsels of maxims, words of wisdom, and powerful plays designed to produce champs. I kept his book from that day to this and cherished every jot and tittle of its wisdom and knowledge.

I believed in conditioning my players. I believed they had to be physically fit to play the game of football. Therefore, my players had to go through the rigorous drill of calisthenics, physical exercises. In order to facilitate that process, I personally made my own weights for the players. Just as they did not pay me a salary for coaching the team, neither did they provide finance for equipment needed for physically conditioning the team. I had to provide that myself.

I persuaded some of the coaches at Chickasaw to join me in making weights out of cans. We took large three gallon cans and filled them with cement. We placed a 36 inch iron pipe in one end and let it settle over night. Once that can settled and the cement became firm, we took another three gallon can and did the same. When we completed the process, we had our own weights. The players could use these to build their muscle mass.

Using these unconventional methods, I provided our players what they needed as a key to achieving a winning season. In addition, I held practice sessions at unconventional hours. While everyone else was asleep, I was out working. I got my boys up on Saturday morning and had them on the practice field at 5 o'clock a.m. We were on the field practicing before daybreak. One morning, one of the boys hit the door and set off the alarm in the school building. The police came and said, "What's going on?" When they saw me and my team, they said, "O Lord, this is that crazy Coach McCray! What in the world you got these boys out here for?" I told them, "We can go over the rules and plays before the sun comes up. When the sun comes up, we can go on the field. We'll be through before 9:00 o'clock in the morning." The policeman said, "You're the craziest woman I have ever seen." I said, "Yea, but I'm going to have a winning team." While all the other coaches were sitting around doing nothing, I was practicing, talking to my players. I always thought if I could control their mind, I had control of my players.

It took a few years for the combinations I put together to begin to work. I diligently integrated Coach Hosea Alexander's philosophy into my coaching style and philosophy. I took some of Coach Bear Bryant's style and philosophy and integrated it into my own. I took a little from here and a little from there and it all began to jell. In 1978, I reached the zenith of accomplishments in producing a winning team. My Chickasaw team went undefeated.

From 1973 till 1978, I had molded my players into solid athletes. They were solid mentally. They were tough minded. They were tops academically. They had to maintain high grades to remain on the team. In addition, they had to come up to standards as far as physical conditioning and knowledge of plays was concerned. I made the youngsters want to win. And so, without any prior training in the area of football, and without any pay, I accomplished this fete.

By the grace of God, I developed some excellent players. One of whom was Carl Lang, who died of leukemia in 1976. He was the caliber of player I successfully cultivated as I moved them from chumps to champs. Another was my quarterback, Rufus Gunn. He followed me through Junior High and High School years. He was more than a player, he was like a son. He was an excellent quarterback, the best I ever had. He was coachable, never got angry, but followed directions. He could have gone on to become a quarterback on any professional football team. Steve Becton was another outstanding member of that championship team. He was a running back, with the speed of a gazelle. He could really run the ball.

In 1978, my Chickasaw Chieftains went undefeated. We were 5 and 0 and won the South Red League championship. We had a league schedule which looked like the following:

> Lanier
> Westwood
> Hillcrest
> Graceland
> Havenview

The teams we played were all coached by males. They were paid by their school or the Board of Education and had supplies provided by their schools or the Board of Education. In some cases, male coaches were paid from monies raised through the sale of concessions. If their salary was not included in the budget from the Board of Education, this was the way they earned their salary. I was not getting paid in any way. But, what I was doing was so satisfying that at the time, it did not matter.

When I began to win, coaching began to be fun. It was even more so that way when I became aware that I was the first woman to coach an all male football team in the United States. The truth of my being the first woman to coach an all male football team grew out of curiosity. The editor of the Memphis Commercial Appeal wrote a letter to the National Federation of State High School Associations inquiring whether there were on record a woman who had coached an all male football team. Their response was, "As far as we know there is no woman coaching a boys team in the United States." Thus, in 1975, it was confirmed that I was the first and only woman to have such distinction. Becoming aware of this fete, in conjunction with the assistance

Coach McCray and her 1978-79 championship team at Chickasaw Junior High School

I got from Coach Hosea Alexander and so many others, I became charged anew as though I had been the recipient of a double shot of adrenaline. I was rejuvenated in a way that I drove myself as a tyrant. I tirelessly studied, planned, prayed, and coached until I won the first championship for Chickasaw in 1978.

In 1979, my Chickasaw team repeated again as champions of the South Red League. Our opposition was the same schools we had played the previous year:

> Lanier
> Westwood
> Hillcrest
> Graceland
> Havenview

It was a good feeling to know I had brought my team from the basement to the brow of the hill as champions. It was an exciting feeling to know that I had developed a team which out-played all the rest so much so that we claimed championship two years in a row. I could not have felt better. Most importantly was the feeling of my players. They were ecstatic over their accomplishments. I was happy for them. I was happy that they had witnessed for themselves the truth of my philosophy, that if they focused on their goal, maneuvered around the obstacles and kept pushing toward the goal, they would win football games and become champions. All I had taught finally paid off.

When it became known that I was the first woman to coach an all male football team, I did not think too much about it. But, after 1975, when this was established as fact, my popularity began to skyrocket. Especially following my victories which resulted in championship teams in 1978 and 1979, my popularity escalated.

The school librarian at Chickasaw Junior High School, Mrs. Jessie Owens, sent a newspaper clipping from the Memphis Press Scimitar to Ebony Magazine in Chicago, Illinois and informed them of their confirmation that I was the first and only woman to coach an all male football team. We received a correspondence from Ebony stating their interest and that an editorial meeting was scheduled to determine if a story would be written. The letter read:

Ebony
820 South Michigan Avenue
Chicago, Ill. 60605
Charles L. Sanders, Managing Editor

December 1, 1977

Dear Mrs. Owens:
    It was very kind of you to send us the newspaper clipping on Coach Shirley McCray. We will discuss Ms. McCray in an editorial meeting and will be in touch with her if an article is scheduled.
    We appreciate your interest.

Sincerely,
Charles L. Sanders

Mrs. Jessie Owens
Librarian
Chickasaw Junior High School
4060 Westmont
Memphis, Tennessee 38109

CLS:se

Indeed, Ebony moved with dispatch to cover the story. They hired Mr. Walter Levy of Memphis, a sports editor with the Memphis *Press Scimitar*, to do the story. They also hired a photographer from the Memphis *Press Scimitar* to take photographs. A very elaborate article appeared in the December 1978 edition of *EBONY MAGAZINE* entitled, "The Football Coach Is A Lady." The next month, January of 1979, *Jet Magazine* printed another article featuring me and focusing on the fact of me being the first woman in the United States to coach an all male football team. As a result of this article, *EBONY*

Coach McCray during 1978 Championship year at Chickasaw

hired Mr. Levy to become one of their writers. He is now senior managing editor for *EBONY*.

This notoriety was followed by visits from representatives of *Kid's World*, a CBS Television program. Their entire crew came from New York City to Memphis to interview me. They had me to get the team dressed and send the players through some of the drills and plays. They filmed all the activity and had one of my players to interview me.

The *EBONY* article precipitated an avalanche of TV appearances and opportunities to receive accolades. I was invited to Cleveland, Ohio to appear on a program on Channel 5 called *Morning Exchange*. This was a talk show where I was queried about my accomplishments as a woman coach of an all male football team. I was treated royally. They housed me in one of the swankiest hotels in Cleveland, more plush than anything I had been accustomed to.

I was doubly elated when I received a letter from the president of Memphis State University about my accomplishments. I had sent a copy of the article which appeared in the *EBONY MAGAZINE* simply for their information. I never expected to get a response, but I did.

OFFICE OF THE PRESIDENT   DECEMBER 6, 1978

Ms. Shirley McCray
Chickasaw Jr. High School
4060 Westmont
Memphis, TN 38109

Dear Coach McCray:

How nice of you to share with me the article which appeared
in a recent issue of *EBONY*. As the first female coach of a
football team you should take justifiable pride not only in
being the first of a type but also even more pride in the
fact that you are helping to shape the lives of some fine
young men.

My congratulations to you, and my very best wishes for
continued success in your endeavors. We need more
dedicated professionals like you.

Kindest regards,

Billy M. Jones
President

cc: Ms. Elma Roane

In 1979, Operation PUSH cited me as one of the winningest
coaches in Memphis.

I was sitting on the crest of the hill of popularity. A coach's dare
had turned me into the nation's darling. What he did to me as evil was
meant as good by God so I could save many of the young men who
otherwise might have fallen through the cracks of life. In the process
of God using me in such a mighty way, I rose from nothing to notoriety. But the main thing was that I had brought my boys from the basement to the brow of the hill as champions of Junior High School football in Memphis. I had brought them from chumps to champs. They
were proud of their accomplishments. They had been made believers
of what they could become and who they could be by following my

leadership. In all of the hoopla over who I was and what I had accomplished, I was happier for the young fellows more than anything else.

CHAPTER XVI

FLIRTING WITH HOLLYWOOD

The lamb. . .began to follow the wolf
in sheep's clothing.
        The Wolf in Sheep's Clothing
        Aesop

Notoriety has its moments of magic, but its moments of misery as well. When an individual is catapulted to the pinnacle of prominence, he or she consequentially could become a lightning rod to attract momentary electrical charges of excitement, hope, and promise. Quite often, however, those lightning strikes of emotional excitement fizzle disgustingly into broken hopes and shattered dreams. Such was my momentary rendezvous with Hollywood. I received a call from Mr. George Wallach of Hollywood. He claimed to be a movie producer. He came to Memphis and contacted me by phone and said he had read my story in the news and in an article in *EBONY MAGAZINE*. He inquired of my interest in signing a movie contract with him. I told him I was interested but would need to talk with my lawyer. He told me he would be happy to meet with me and lawyer. I said okay and proceeded to arrange a meeting with a lawyer.

I really did not know a lawyer at the time. I had a friend who was a lawyer, but he was a criminal lawyer. I learned later there was a vast difference between criminal lawyers and those who knew contracts dealing with rights, copyrights, movie rights, book rights, and the like. The lawyer I consulted, a Black criminal lawyer from Memphis, was the man I selected to assist me. The gentleman from California met with me and my attorney. We talked about a contract to do a movie of some sort on my life. We listened to him and delivered a volley of questions in search of answers to our questions concerning his request. He talked persuasively and found in us two sets of eager, listening ears. He left assuring that a contract would soon follow. It did.

As of July 24, 1979

Ms. Shirley McCray
c/o Walter Bailey, Esq.
161 Jefferson, Suite 901
Memphis, Tennessee 38103

Dear Ms. McCray:

This will confirm the agreement and understanding between the undersigned, WALLACH PRODUCTIONS, a division of Sports Media Sales, Inc. ("Purchaser"), and you ("McCray") with respect to the acquisition by Purchaser of certain Rights (as hereinafter defined).

1.   In consideration of the sum of Two Hundred Fifty Dollars ($250.00), receipt of which is hereby acknowledged, McCray grants to Purchaser the exclusive and irrevocable right and option (the "Option"), but not the obligation to purchase all of the Rights, as hereinafter defined. The Option may be exercised by Purchaser by written notice at any time during the period (the "option period") of one (1) year from and after the date hereof. The option period may be extended for an additional consecutive one (1) year period (the "first extension") by the payment to McCray of an additional sum of Five Hundred Dollars ($500.00) at any time prior to the expiration of the initial Option Period. The option period may be further extended for an additional consecutive one (1) year period (the "second extension") by the payment to McCray of an additional sum of Five Hundred Dollars ($500.00) at any time prior to the expiration of the first extension.

2.   If Purchaser shall exercise the Option hereunder, the payments set forth in Paragraph 1 hereof will apply and be credited against the first sums payable as total consideration for the Rights, as follows:
(a)   Twenty Thousand Dollars ($20,000.00) payable on exercise (if ever) of the Option; and
(b)   If Purchaser produces a feature-length motion picture based on the Property, as hereinafter defined (the "Picture"), an amount equal to two and one-half percent (2-1/2%)

112

of Purchaser's share of the net profits derived from the Picture.

(i)   As used herein, "Purchaser's share of the net profits" shall mean 100% of the net profits payable to Purchaser in connection with the Picture less all participations in the receipts and profits of the Picture payable to all third parties.

(ii)   As used herein, the term "net profits" shall mean net profits or equivalent term as computed and accounted for in accordance with the distribution or similar agreement entered into by Purchaser with a third party (either separately or as a joint venturer) relating to the distribution and/or exploitation of the Picture.   Whenever Purchaser shall receive from third parties payments remitted as net profits of the Picture, Purchaser shall remit to McCray not later than thirty (30) days after receipt by Purchaser of such payment, McCray's percentage of the net profits out of the sums so remitted by third parties to Purchaser, and Purchaser shall, with such payment to McCray, enclose a copy of the statement rendered by third parties which shall accompany said remittance to Purchaser. Purchaser shall be obligated to pay McCray's percentage of the net profits only out of sums actually received by Purchaser as net profits of the Picture, and not otherwise; and in no event shall Purchaser be obligated to make any payments to McCray hereunder if third parties shall default or be in breach of their obligations to make payments to Purchaser out of the net profits of the Picture.

(iii)   McCray shall look solely to Purchaser for the payment of McCray's percentage of the Purchaser's share of the net profits and McCray further acknowledges that McCray shall not be entitled to any separate statements of accounting from third parties. If the distributor of the Picture or other appropriate third party agrees to pay McCray's share of the net profits and render statements and otherwise account directly to McCray in connection with the Picture, Purchaser shall be relieved of all liability in connection with such payments, statements and accounting. McCray shall be barred from maintaining or instituting any action or proceeding based upon or relating to any statement or accounting made by Purchaser or any third party acting under the authority of Purchaser to McCray with respect to McCray's share of the net profits derived from the distribution and exploitation of the Picture unless written objection shall have been delivered to Purchaser within twelve (12) months from and after the mailing of such statement or accounting, and unless such action or proceeding is commenced within six (6) months after the delivery of such written objection. Notwithstanding anything to the contrary contained in the immediately preceding sentence, if the aforesaid distribution agreement provides for a shorter period of time for making objections to a statement or accounting or for commencing an action or proceeding, as the case may be, than that set forth in the immediately preceding sentence, then, unless McCray's share of the net profits is being paid directly to McCray by the distributor or other appropriate third person party to the distribution agreement with Purchaser, the twelve (12) month and six (6) month periods shall be reduced to one (1) month less than the time provided for in such distribution agreement.

(iv)   McCray agrees that in the event of any breach of Purchaser's obligations to make payment to McCray pursuant to this Subparagraph 2(b), McCray's sole remedy will be an action at law against Purchaser for damages, and McCray acknowledges that McCray shall not have the right to institute any proceedings to enjoin or restrain the production, exhibition, or distribution of the Picture, nor the right to rescind, cancel, or revoke this agreement, nor any of the rights, privileges or benefits granted to Purchaser hereunder.

114

(v)   If Purchaser shall sell or otherwise dispose of the Picture to any so-called "major" studio or distributor of motion pictures or other financially responsible party who undertakes to pay the amounts payable to McCray as provided in this agreement, Purchaser shall be relieved from any further obligation or liability to McCray with respect to such payments.

(vi)   Purchaser does not represent that the Picture, if produced, will be released, nor, if released, that there will be any net profits. Nothing contained herein shall obligate Purchaser to make, produce, release, distribute, advertise, or exploit the Picture.

(vii)   Nothing contained in this agreement shall be construed so as to require all or any of the proceeds from the Picture to be held in trust by Purchaser for McCray or to impose upon Purchase any fiduciary obligations to McCray and nothing contained in this agreement shall constitute a partnership between or a joint venture by the parties hereto. McCray shall have no right, title or interest in or to the Picture.

(viii)   In the event that Purchaser shall not enter into a distribution agreement relating to the Picture containing a definition of net profits, then net profits shall mean and amount equal to the excess, if any, of the gross receipts (as such gross receipts are customarily defined in the motion picture and television industries in Los Angeles, California) actually received by Purchaser from the distribution and exploitation of the Picture in the United States in U. S. Dollars over the aggregate of the following, which shall be deducted in the order listed:

(A)   Purchaser's distribution fees, as are customary in the motion picture and television industries;

(B)   The aggregate of the costs and

115

expenses incurred in connection with the distribution, advertising, exploitation and turning to account of the Picture of whatever kind of nature, or which are customarily treated as distribution expenses in the motion picture and television industries;

(C)   The total cost of production of the Picture, plus interest thereon at the then prevailing prime commercial rate plus two percent (2%) (with said interest to be recouped before the cost of production);

(D)   All contingent amounts (including, without limitation, deferments) payable to third parties not included in the cost of production;

(E)   All third party participations in the gross receipts and net profits of the Picture.

Purchaser shall render to McCray periodic statements and payments, if any shall be due, in the manner and form as is customary in the motion picture industry, and the interest on the cost of production shall accrue in accordance with customary practice in the motion picture and television industries.

3.   (a) Purchaser shall exercise reasonable efforts to prepare a proposal suitable for presentation to the ABC, CBS, and/or NBC television networks in an effort to secure a financing commitment for the development of the Picture, within the period of six (6) months from and after the date hereof.
(b) Purchaser shall make a presentation to at least two of the three U. S. television networks in an effort to secure a financing commitment for the development of the picture. If Purchaser both (i) fails to make such presentations and (ii) fails to secure a financing commitment, during the option period, Purchaser shall have no right to extend the option period hereunder.

(c) If Purchaser makes the presentations referred to in Paragraph 3(b) above during the initial option period, but nonetheless both (i) has not secured a financing commitment from one of the networks, and (ii) has not engaged the services of a writer for the preparation of an outline, treatment, story and/or teleplay based on all or any portion of the Rights, prior to the expiration of the option period, the payment for the first extension provided in Paragraph 1 above shall be One Thousand Dollars ($1,000.00), rather than Five Hundred Dollars ($500.00).

4.　　　As used herein, the "Rights" shall be defined as the sole, exclusive and perpetual right to portray, dramatize, fictionalize, represent and exploit the life story of McCray and/or any part thereof, including, without limitation the sole, exclusive and perpetual theatrical motion picture, television and allied and incidental rights in and to the life of McCray and any and all accounts thereof, whether written, photographic, oral or in any other form (the "Property"), together with any and all screenplays or other adaptations thereof whether heretofore or hereafter written by McCray or any other person, in all languages throughout the universe, including, without limitation, theatrical, television (whether filmed, taped or otherwise recorded, and including series rights), cassette and other compact devices, remake and advertising and promotion rights (including 10,000 word excerpt and summary publication rights); all rights to exploit, distribute and exhibit any motion picture or other production produced hereunder in all media now known or hereafter devised; all rights to make any and all changes to and adaptations of the Property; merchandising, commercial tie-up, sound track, music publishing and exploitation rights;　the right to use McCray's name in and in connection with the exploitation of the rights granted hereunder; and all other rights customarily obtained in connection with formal rights acquisition agreements, including, without limitation, the sole and exclusive right to obtain copyright and other protection for any and all exploitation of the Property by Purchaser hereunder.

5.　　　(a) McCray hereby represents and warrants that: (i) McCray is the owner of the Rights herein conveyed free and clear of any liens, encumbrances, claims or litigation, whether pending or threatened; (ii) neither the Property nor any element thereof nor any exploitation of the Rights by Purchaser hereunder does or will infringe upon or violate the rights of privacy or publicity of any person or constitute a defamation of any person or infringe upon or violate any rights of any kind or nature whatsoever of any person whomsoever; (iii) McCray has full right and power to make and perform this agreement and to grant all of the rights granted herein without limitation or restriction; (iv) no part of the Property herein conveyed has previously been used or exploited, as a motion picture, television production, or play; and no rights have been granted to any third party to do so; (v) neither the Property nor any part thereof has ever been published or has ever been registered for copyright in the United States of America or elsewhere; (vi) McCray shall obtain and deliver to Purchaser all consents, permissions, and releases required from third parties to enable Purchaser fully to exploit the Rights as set forth herein; and (vii) McCray shall defend, indemnify and hold harmless Purchaser and Purchaser's licensees, agents, assigns and associates, if any, from and against any and all claims, demands, charges, damages, costs, expenses (including without limitation, attorney's fees and legal costs, whether or not in connection with litigation), judgments, penalties, liabilities or losses of any kind or nature whatsoever by reason of, relating to or arising out of any matter or thing constituting, or alleged to constitute, a breach of any of McCray's covenants, representations or warranties set forth in this agreement.

(b)   All of the rights, licenses, privileges and properties herein granted to Purchaser are irrevocable and are not subject to rescission, restraint or injunction under any and all circumstances. McCray hereby waives the so-called "moral rights" of authors in connection with the Property and Purchaser's exploitation thereof hereunder.

(c)   Prior to Purchaser's exercise of the Option, if ever, Purchaser may engage in development and preproduction activities in connection with the exploitation of the Rights, including, without limitation, the preparation and submission of treatments, screenplays and teleplays based upon the Property. The results and proceeds of all such development

118

and preproduction activities shall remain the sole and exclusive property of Purchaser notwithstanding Purchaser's failure to exercise the Option.

6.   All notices and payments from Purchaser to McCray shall be sent to McCray in care of Walter Bailey, Esq., 161 Jefferson, Suite 901, Memphis, Tennessee 38103; all notices from McCray to Purchaser shall be sent to Wallach Productions, a division of Sports Media Sales, Inc., 1901 Avenue of the Stars, Los Angeles, California 90067, Attention: George Wallach, with a copy to: Manatt, Phelps, Rothenberg and Tunney, 1888 Century Park East, Suite 2100, Los Angeles, California 90067, Attention: Fredric I. Bernstein, Esq. Either party hereto may change its address by written notice given to the other party. All notices shall be given by depositing the same, postage prepaid, certified, return receipt requested, in the United States mail; or by delivering the same personally; or by delivering the same, toll prepaid, to a telegraph or cable company. Any notice shall be deemed given when so deposited in the mail, personally delivered or so delivered to a telegraph or cable company, as the case may be.

7.   It is hereby agreed and acknowledged that the rights granted to Purchaser herein are of a special, unique, unusual, extraordinary and intellectual character, giving them peculiar value, the loss of which cannot be reasonably or adequately compensated in damages in an action at law; a breach by McCray of any of the provisions hereof would cause Purchaser irreparable injury and damage. Accordingly, in the event of McCray's breach of the provisions hereof, Purchaser shall be entitled to specific performance and injunctive relief and such other equitable relief which may be appropriate; Purchaser's resort to any such equitable relief shall not be construed as or be deemed to be a waiver of any other rights and remedies to which Purchaser may be entitled at law for damages or otherwise.

8.   Notwithstanding anything herein to the contrary, in the event of any breach of or default under the provisions hereof by Purchaser, McCray's sole remedy shall be to seek damages in a court of competent jurisdiction, and in no

event shall McCray be entitled to obtain any injunctive or other equitable relief or undertake any legal efforts to restrict Purchaser's right to exploit the Rights.

9.   In the event that any action, suit or proceeding arising from or based upon this agreement is brought by either party hereto against the other, in addition to all other remedies at law or as herein provided, the prevailing party shall be entitled to recover from the other party its attorney's fees in connection therewith in addition to the costs of the action, suit or proceeding, whether or not prosecuted to judgment.

10.   This agreement supersedes and replaces all agreements (oral or written) between McCray and Purchaser relating to the Property. This agreement, including all of the foregoing provisions and all exhibits made a part hereof, expresses the entire understanding and agreement of the parties hereto and replaces any and all prior agreements and understandings, whether written or oral, relating in any way to the subject matter of this agreement. This agreement cannot be modified, amended or supplemented except by a written instrument or instruments executed by each of the parties hereto. This agreement shall be construed and enforced in accordance with the laws of the State of California applicable to contracts entered into and wholly performed in such state. Purchaser shall have the irrevocable and unrestricted right to assign this agreement to any person, firm or corporation. McCray shall not have the right to assign or transfer any of your rights hereunder, and any attempted assignment or transfer by McCray contrary to the terms hereof shall be null and void. Subject to the foregoing, this agreement shall be binding upon and inure to the benefit of the parties hereto and their successors, representatives, assigns and licensees.

11.   Nothing contained in this agreement shall be construed so as to (a) require the commission of any act of the payment of any compensation which is contrary to law or (b) require the violation of any collective bargaining agreement between Purchaser its licensees and assigns, if any, and any guild, union or other labor organization which may, from

time to time, be in effect and by its terms controlling with respect to this agreement. Whenever there is any conflict between this agreement and any applicable law or any collective bargaining agreement applicable hereto, the applicable law, or collective bargaining agreement, as the case may be, shall prevail, and the provision(s) of this agreement affected shall be modified to the extent, but only to the extent, necessary to remove said conflict and permit compliance with such law, or collective bargaining agreement, as the case may be, and, as so modified, this agreement shall remain in full force and effect.

Yours very truly,
WALLACH PRODUCTIONS,
a Division of Sports Media Sales, Inc.

By_____

Its_____

ACCEPTED AND AGREED TO:

_____

SHIRLEY McCRAY

My attorney and I went over this contract with Mr. Wallach. I thought we went over it rather carefully. I did not know much about contracts and its reading seemed rather complex, vague, and confusing. It really was a labyrinthine maze of juridical gibberish, professional prattle, and entangling obtusities which left me baffled. There seemed to be some agreement between Mr. Wallach and the lawyer assisting me to be sure I understood what the contract was saying. Neither one helped me know what the contract said, but it sounded good to hear that I could get some money, not much I must admit, for having my life's accomplishments flashed across a screen throughout the nation. Thus, I left it to my lawyer to understand all about the contractual contortions that I had just read. I took the $250.00 offered by the Hollywood representative with a feeling of assurance that everything was okay and that more would come.

After the gentleman's departure, I felt an uneasy confidence. I only hoped he would call with a follow-up to our meeting. I did not hear from him at all. He had persuaded me to think of him as a man of integrity. He insisted that he was the representative for Bruce Jenner, a star I had heard of. He boasted rather strongly that he had secured sports advertisement contracts for Jenner. He assured me that he could do the same for me. That sounded good to me.

After some time passed, I was consumed by a gargantuan appetite of curiosity, I called this Mr. Wallach to see what was gong on. I was finally successful in reaching him. He told me things were not progressing and that I should give him more time to get things arranged. I continued to call, he gave me one excuse after another. After about two years, he gave me the excuse that he could not find anyone to play my part. He said he had asked Cicely Tyson but she declined, saying she did not have the personality to play my part. With my senses bristling with vibrating anxiety, I shot back, "I can play my own part." He said in a matter-of-factly, business-like manner, arresting my rising tone of voice, "I want to get somebody famous because that will get your movie up off the ground and people will want to come and look at it." We went back and forth, on and on and on like this for some time. I could not get any clarity or sense of direction from this Hollywood representative.

Three years of this going back and forth passed without any development, or so I thought. My colleague, fellow teacher, and friend, Dollie Scruggs, wrote letters to all major movie producers encouraging them to consider my story as a movie. She sent copies to Warner Brothers, Walt Disney Productions, and the like:

Sept. 6th 1984

From: Dollie Scruggs
1022 University
Memphis, Tennessee

To: All Interested producers,

I'm sitting here looking at a movie about Shirley Muldowney, woman race car driver, and I'm wondering why a movie can't be made about Shirley McCray, first woman football coach.

Shirley McCray, junior high school teacher and coach has been coaching boys' football since 1974 - ten years. She has received some recognition in EBONY and Jet Magazines - Dec. 1978. Also through local newspapers and television shows. She also appeared on Kids World in 1980.

122

*This is a great lady with a great story. I can't tell you
all about her in this letter. Her story would make
a great movie or television series. 1984 is the year of
the woman. Please don't let this year pass without considering a movie or series about this lady.*

*To learn more about her, contact her and come and see her
in action. Lanier Jr. High School - 817 Brownlee Rd. -
Memphis, Tn. 38116.*

Friend and co-worker,
Dollie Scruggs

*P.S. Football was removed from junior high schools in
Memphis in 1981 due to finances. It's being reinstated
this school year (84-85). The present principal at Chickasaw
Jr. High would not allow Ms. McCray to coach football -
why??? Right! because she's a woman. Therefore,
she transferred to Lanier Jr. High where she is presently
coaching football.*

Although this letter was sent to many movie producers in Hollywood,
only Walt Disney Productions sent a response with regrets, saying I
needed an agent. Warner Brothers did not respond, and for a good reason.

I received a call from my brother in Chicago. That call brought
with it a great deal of reason for concern. From the other end, my
brother said to me, "Shirley, you'd better get up here. We have learned
that Warner Bros. from Hollywood is in Chicago making a movie about
a woman football coach with an all male team." My brother was an
assistant coach at one of the high schools in Chicago. The word had
gotten around about the movie because Warner Bros., was using the
football field of one of the schools in the city. The rumor mill ground
out the news of their presence. Alarmed at what I was hearing, I said,
"They can't do that!" Insult began to boil into anger, anger gave way to
rage, and finally, rage succumbed to hurt and indescribable pain. I
shouted into the phone, "That man who is supposed to be my agent
told me that nobody could take my name or what I am about and make
a movie without contacting him."

I slammed the phone into its cradle, looking at it blankly, with a
dazed feeling, numbed, and dumbfounded. I picked up the phone
again and dialed Mr. Wallach in California. Fortunately, I reached him.

I tried to maintain my composure, but my voice was trembling and the phone was shaking in my hand. I said, "Did you know that Warner Bros., is in Chicago making a movie about a lady football coach and an all male team?" He said calmly and matter-of-factly but with a modicum of measured excitement, "Oh no, they can't do that. Warner Brothers ain't doing that. They can't do that." I said to him, "Aren't you a movie producer?" He said, "Yea, that's why I know they ain't doing that." I said, "Sir, they are in Chicago and I am on my way up there." Incredibly he said to me, "Call me when you get there." I couldn't believe he said that to me. If he were concerned, I thought, he should have been on his way to Chicago to accompany me.

I took off for Chicago. When I arrived, I immediately sought out the truth of my brother's phone call. Indeed, I discovered that Warner Brothers had been in town making a movie about a woman football coach and an all male team. They had just completed shooting the scenes. My brother was right. My cousin, Dorothy, suggested that I secure a lawyer. She said she knew of a Jewish lawyer who was good. "If anybody can get something done for you, this man can."

I immediately made an appointment and went down town and met with him. When I told him of the situation, he said, "Oh yes, these folk have stolen your idea." I showed him the article which appeared in EBONY MAGAZINE and Jet. He beamed, "Yea, honey, you ought to get some money off of this, at least a hundred thousand dollars. They really used you." I hired him to be my lawyer to handle the case. I left his office with measured confidence that justice would be done. I went back to Memphis thinking that I was in for a large sum of money from that movie.

For three months, I called and called that lawyer. I worried him, trying to get something done. Nothing happened. Finally, I received a nice long letter from him stating that his wife had gotten sick and he was compelled to drop the case. He informed me that he was relocating, moving to Arizona.

I sought to hire a lawyer in Memphis to help me. I went to Elvis Presley's lawyer. Immediately he asked for $10,000.00 in advance. He said he needed that kind of money for depositions and other exploratory work. Rising up from my seat in his office, I mildly shouted at him with strong voice and a rigid visage, "Where am I going to get that kind of money? Man, where am I going to get $10,000? I am a poor teacher!" He whirled in his chair and said, rising up from where he was sitting, "Sell some of those houses you've got. Sell some of them." I said, "Nooo! If you say I can get some money out of this, then you wait till I get some money!" After that meeting, that lawyer started to dodge me.

I went to another lawyer, then another, then another. One after another, they all listened to my case and concluded that I had a good case. They all initially agreed to take the case. But after about two months, I heard no more from them. I felt they had been paid off. I do not know what happened to them. All I know is, after probing into the case, each one politely backed off and then out of the picture.

The more I looked into the matter, the more I concluded that I had made the error at the very beginning. The Hollywood representative had fashioned a contract that was so complex and unfamiliar to the novice lawyer, one who had not trafficked in the vernacular of Hollywood, that he could smooth over the tricks and traps hidden therein. My lawyer, because he had been paid by Mr. Wallach to interpret the contract to me to his/our satisfaction, became as it were a silent conspirator, because of his lack of knowledge of contractual law. I was duped into thinking I would make money. What I agreed to was to allow WAllACH PRODUCTIONS to take my unique story and make a movie out of it without any obligation to me. The contract made no provisions for recourse on my part. The representative went back to Los Angeles with what he came for, a *CARTE BLANCHE* approval to make use of my story and make money from it with no threat of legal suit on my part.

This hundred percent hindsight surfaced long after the fact of my error and omission. After much pain and soul-searching, I concluded that there was nothing I could do. I forgot about the whole thing.

Sure enough, months after all this happened, Hollywood came out with the movie entitled, *GOLDIE HAWN AND THE WILDCATS*. The leading role was played by a white actress, Goldie Hawn. It was the depiction of a woman who coached an all male football team. A co-worker and long-time friend, Dollie Scruggs, wrote a letter to *People Weekly*, a magazine, and poignantly expressed my sentiments.

1022 University St.
Memphis, Tenn.
August 20th, 1986.

<u>*People Weekly*</u>
Time Inc.
c/o Linda Witt, Bureau Chief
303 East Ohio Street
Chicago, Illinois,

Dear Ms. Witt,

I'm writing this letter in behalf of Coach Shirley McCray-first woman football coach of an all male team. Shirley did not coach for a few years because it was taken out of junior high school in Memphis for financial reasons. Football is back and so is Coach McCray. She is presently coaching football in high school-junior varsity head coach. She's at Booker T. Washington high school-which is located in a high poverty and crime area.

I wrote a letter similar to this one about Coach McCray to Warner Bros. Productions in Sept. of 1984. Two months later, Warner Bros. began filming *"Goldie Hawn and the Wildcats"*. The movie is about a woman football coach. Many of the episodes in the movie are very similar to the things that I stated about Coach McCray in the letter. I, nor Coach McCray ever received a reply of any kind from Warner Bros. I'm not saying that Warner Bros. stole the idea, but that it's very strange that a movie was produced by Warner Bros. so soon after I sent a letter to them about Coach McCray. There is even something strange about the name of the leading character in the movie (the woman football coach). Her name is Polly McGrath. It seems like my first name, which is Dollie was changed to Polly and Coach McCray's last name was changed to McGrath — Polly McGrath! There are a lot of strange similarities like this concerning this movie. I can understand if you don't want to print this story because of liable reasons. Stating strange similarities and circumstances about something shouldn't be a cause for liable - should it??

I feel Coach McCray's story should be known - if not the full story, then certainly that part about her being the real first woman football coach of an all male team.
If you want to know more about Coach McCray, contact her at:
Booker T. Washington High School
715 South Lauderdale Street
Memphis, Tennessee 38126
Phone: (901) 274-0289

Friend and co-worker,
Sincerely,
Dollie R. Scruggs

My friend Dollie never got a response to her letter. We seemed unable to get anyone to take up our cause. We decided to leave it all alone until I could tell my own story.

CHAPTER XVII

DISCRIMINATION, ELIMINATION, JUSTIFICATION

And ain't I a Woman?
Sojourner Truth

Life taught me some powerfully painful lessons. I learned that you can experience double jeopardy if you are both Black and a woman. At Memphis State University, I suffered discrimination because I was Black. When I became a coach, I suffered discrimination because I was a woman.

My coaching career reached its zenith in 1978 and 1979 when I won back-to-back championships with my teams at Chickasaw Junior High School. Nothing could surpass the euphoria I enjoyed during those two years. Like Richard Bach's Jonathan Livingston Seagull, I soared into the limitless heights of greatness. I left other seagulls by the seashore fighting over crumbs of insignificance and rose to unprecedented heights to soar in corridors where travellers are seen only now and then. I was the nation's, and probably the world's, first woman to coach an all male football team. Unpaid, previously unknown, but there I was basking in the sunlight on the towering peak of prominence. My brow was crowned with gilded garlands for having developed two championship teams.

So quickly however, the storm clouds gathered about me and the atmosphere within the school community turned turbid. So quickly, however, conditions tumbled me from the towering heights of mastery to the turbid nadir of misery. Mysteriously, the advent of the 1980 school year brought with it a seeming contrived budget shortfall which made school administrators rule out football for Junior High Schools in the Memphis Public School System. Just like that, with a casual decision and the stroke of a pen, football was eliminated from the sports program in Memphis City Schools. I could not believe this was happening. One moment, I was standing tiptoe on the mount of prominence and popularity, the next I was plummeted to the pit of despair. My life was rendered empty, void, without the love of my life, football for the young boys I loved to train and see developed in fullness of athletic ability and academic potential. It did not matter that I was unpaid for my coaching duties, I was enjoying every moment of it. I was seeing young boys' lives turned around. I was making a contribution, making young boys believe in themselves. Many of them already were showing promise of becoming assets to society. And so, with the dismissal of Junior High School football, I reckoned that of necessity I was constrained to launch a vigorous warfare against that action.

I began my campaign by attending school board meetings each Monday night. I took a parent with me or I took a football player with me. Each week I sought to appear before the school board so I could set before its members my request to restore football to the school system's sports program. I could not get male coaches to attend and assist my cause. I wrote them, along with principals, a passionate letter to appeal to reason:

MEMO TO
PRINCIPALS & COACHES

FROM
COACH SHIRLEY McCRAY

I am one of the many coaches who wish the board members would take another look at their budget in order to reinstate Junior High School football.

As many of you may know, I am the first woman football coach in the United States, and I coach at Chickasaw Jr. High School. I have, for the past eight years, seen the pros and cons of not having a sound football program. Some of you, if you stop and think back to your school years, realize that the strongest program in the school was your football program. The physical, mental, and spiritual strengths gained in a sound football program carry over into basketball, track and baseball — and, to a great extent, make possible, their survival, since the same young men usually participate in all of them at the junior high level.

Have you ever stopped to think about why basketball is slowly becoming a top sport? It's because of the emphasis placed on it at an early stage. Football, too, can remain a top sport — but only if we will work hard to keep it that way.

I was looking at the NCAA game recently, and was thinking

of how many young men who were playing got their beginnings in junior high school. I'm sure many of them did. The same is true in football, many young men who begin in junior high go on to play college and professional football.

Have you ever thought about the devastation that could occur in the high school football program if the junior high program is not reinstated? The responsibility of teaching the basics in football will fall on the high school coaches — for they will not have players who have been seasoned at an earlier stage — junior high school. Their jobs will be much more difficult. The caliber of players will have declined. Many young athletes, who have not been given the opportunity to develop their abilities in junior high school, will lose out on their chances to play in senior high school. Thus, the senior high football program will be greatly weakened.

The response I received from the principals and coaches was alarming. They said I did not know what I was talking about. This kind of intensively negative opinion became protracted over a long period of time. It took four years, in fact, before we could claim the victory.

During the interim period, I busied myself coaching football and basketball in a Park Commission League in the Westwood section of Memphis. The home base for the team I developed was the community center which served the Westwood community. This was low-paid activity, $3.75 an hour, but it fulfilled my heart's desire of coaching all boys in football and basketball.

I was faced with a peculiar situation in the park commission league. The players I was forced to utilize were rejects and leftovers from high school teams. They had gone out for teams at the high school level but had been dropped because they did not measure up to their standard. I tried to make use of them anyway. This was where I really had to show my coaching prowess. I had to knock off the rough places and hone those young men to a sharp edge. I did not throw any player away.

Cheyenne Gibson was typical of this kind of player. He tried out for the basketball and football high school teams and was rejected. He had long arms, long hands, and big feet. He was a 7th grader and only stood four or five feet. High school coaches simply did not want this player. He was too short, too skinny. High school coaches wanted six footers with a whole lot of skill in the game. You had to be exceptional to play on their teams.

But my style of coaching was that I did not turn anybody down. I took onto my team young boys who were diminutive in physical stature. I did not cut short people, slow people. Whichever way they came was the way I took them. So, I was coaching rejects and developing rejects. But, out of those rejects I built championship teams in the Memphis Park Commission League.

I took young men and taught them not only the skill of the game of football but confidence in themselves. I gave them pride in what they did. Back in those days, if you did not have the natural skill to play the game, other coaches did not want you. They did not take the time to develop the raw talent. They wanted instant success. I took the time to develop that raw talent. I was willing to wait and develop that skill and develop that talent. That is what made me successful. I never turned down anybody.

That is what happened in the case of Cheyenne Gibson. He fooled everybody. That young man came onto my team and outworked everyone. He came to practice and worked hard everyday. He became one of the best players I ever coached. In fact, he became the best player Memphis had ever seen. He went to Memphis State University and completed his schooling there. He played on the basketball team and was one of the greatest players ever to play for Memphis State. He went on to play professional basketball overseas.

My continued pursuit for excellence on the football team yielded the sweet fruit of victory in many other ways aside from a win on the field. I continued to receive accolades and recognition for my accomplishments. In 1982, I was cited as **Coach Of The Year** by the Memphis Park Commission. I was as proud of that accomplishment as any I had previously received. *REAL WORLD SPORTS*, a sports magazine, did a feature article on me entitled, *"She's A New Kind Of Football Coach."* The Memphis *COMMERCIAL APPEAL* newspaper did a story on me in 1982, just as it had in 1978. That same year, I was cited by Sheriff Gene Barksdale as Honorary Deputy Sheriff. The next year, November 30, 1983, I was cited as **Teacher of The Day** by Radio Station WKDJ and Diet Coke.

All the time I coached football and basketball in the Memphis Park Commission League, I continued to keep up the hectic pace of appearing before the Board of Education to appeal to them to restore football in Junior High Schools. I continued to maintain my full schedule of activities at my church, St. Jude Baptist Church. I taught Sunday school. I sang in two choirs, often travelling in the city and outside as well to make singing engagements. I cared for my aunt. I continued to perform any number of life's assignments. But, each Monday evening I was before that Board of Education making my appeal.

In the course of time, a young man named Ricky Peete came to my house and said he wanted to be on the board of education. He made a proposal that if I supported him in his effort to get elected, he would help me get football back into the school system. He assured me that he knew how to write proposals and if he were elected, he would write a proposal that would successfully place football back into the school system.

I took him up on the offer. I helped in his campaign, and, he was elected. Once a member of the board of education, Ricky Peete was true to his word. He wrote a proposal which showed how money could be saved and still have a program of football in junior high schools. In spite of the opposition I experienced in previous appearances, Ricky Peete's proposal

Shirley McCray sings at one of the church functions which always kept her busy. She sings "Give Me My Flowers" at an appreciation dinner for Pastor J.S. White of St. Jude.

was successful. And so after four years, junior high school football was placed back in the Memphis City School System. In a very real sense, this victory rivaled any I had experienced on the football field.

In spite of the victory before the Board of Education in 1984, jealousy, that Shakespearean "Green-eyed Monster," reared its head before me once again. There were 22 head football coaching positions open in Junior High Schools in Memphis. I applied for one of those positions. I was unsuccessful. This was the beginning of my legal quarrel with the Memphis City School System. It was my opinion that I was qualified to be appointed as one of those head football coaching positions. The reason I did not get appointed as a coach was simple — I was a woman! My aggressiveness, my determination to be somebody — the very stuff my grandmother instilled in me — kept wanting to come out. My inner drive would not allow me to sit passively by while they dealt me this injustice. It was in my mind that something had to be done.

To appease me for awhile, I was offered an assistant coaching position at Lanier Junior High School in the Fall of 1984. Reluctantly I took the position with a wary eye and wondering what happened that I could not get the head coaching position. I knew it was a clear cut case of sex discrimination. But for the moment, I settled in for the season. After all, the school board was forced to pay me now, the first time in my

Championship team at Lanier Junior High School, 1984-85.

coaching career I would receive pay for what I did; that was some consolation.

Indeed, my skill as a coach, albeit functioning as an assistant at Lanier, proved fruitful. Working alongside Coach Roosevelt Hodges at Lanier, we produced a championship team in 1984 for our 9th grade team and our 7th and 8th grade team. In 1985, we tied with Chickasaw Junior High School and ended the season as Co-champions. Our 7th and 8th grade team completed the season as champions. We were proud of our accomplishments.

In the Fall of 1986, the lid literally blew off the keg of sexual discrimination. The principal at Lanier Junior High School, Mr. Dorsey T. Patterson requested that I accompany him along with Coach Roosevelt Hodges to Booker T. Washington High School. He had been assigned there as the new principal. He invited me to accompany him and I became the head junior varsity football coach and girls track and assistant girls basketball coach with Coach Eva Bass. I was elated at his invitation and jumped at the offer. But, my arrival at Booker T. Washington High School was when my real problems began.

It was soon discovered by the male coaching staff at Booker T. Washington that the coach of the junior varsity team was a woman. In concert and fierce calculation, the male coaching staff attacked me with the intention of driving me from my job. When I showed up on the field to assume my coaching duties, I was approached by an assistant coach of the boys team. He wasted no time in getting his point over to me and making it clear that he did not want to be associated with me in the business of coaching. He caustically said to me, "The football field is no place for a woman." I swallowed hard to abate the lump which rose annoyingly in my throat. I fought the rush of adrenaline which caused my fists to clutch tightly and my body to stiffen, as if for war. I was slowly getting angry, but I remembered Rudyard Kipling's poetic truth,

If you can keep your head,
When all about you are losing theirs
And blaming it on you;
If you can trust yourself
When all men doubt you,
But make allowance for their doubting too;
If you can wait
And not be tired by waiting,
Or being lied about, don't deal in lies,
Or being hated, don't give way to hating,
And yet don't look too good, nor talk too wise;

If you can dream,
And not make dreams your master;
If you can think,
And not make thoughts your aim;
If you can deal with Triumph and Disaster,
And treat those two impostors just the same;
If you can bear to hear the truth you've spoken
Twisted by knaves to make a trap for fools,
Or watch the things you gave your life to — broken
And stoop and build 'em up with worn out tools.

If you can talk with crowds
And not lose your virtue,
Or walk with kings nor lose the common touch;
If neither foes or loving friends can hurt you;
And all men count with you — but none too much;
If you can fill the unforgiving minute
Sixty seconds, of long distance run,
Yours is the world and everything that's in it,
And which is more, you'll be a Man, my son!

My persistence kept pushing me onto the field each day. And, each day abuse and embarrassment met me forthrightly. The coach continued his verbal volley of obscenities and lashings with his lethal lip. He cursed and berated me, often before fellow coaches and play ers. In fact, during a game one of the football players inadvertently ran up to me to ask directions about a game situation. Overhearing what was happening, the coach rushed over and grabbed the player in the chest. Screaming obscenities and other impurities of language, Mr. Hodges said to the young man, "Don't ask her a '@ @ # #' thing! She can't coach! Ask me, '@ # & * @' !" This constant encounter and irreverent rendezvous grew in intensity as the days passed. Tension grew thicker each day, not only between me and the male coaches, but between the players and the male coaches as well. The players were struggling with how to deal with their hostile feelings which were surfacing because of the way I was being treated.

The caustic condition continued and grew to a head. One day the assistant coach's verbal abuse and obscene confrontation reached the pits. He said to me, "You need to take your '---' inside and wash clothes and clean up the locker room and be glad to get paid for that." I was stunned. I was hurt. I was numbed and my brains sizzled with the electricity of shock. Blood rushed to my eyes and my physical powers employed tears to wash it away so I could see. I thought maybe the head coach would intercede and mitigate the moment for me. But no! In support of the assistant coach, the head coach proceeded to assign me to the locker room to wash clothes and clean up. Washing clothes and cleaning the locker room was my assignment for the remainder of the year.

I conceded to the embarrassing assignment because the coaches were my superiors. However, on October 25, 1986, I wrote a letter to the principal, citing the incidents which had happened. I sent a copy of the letter to the superintendent of schools, which at the time was Dr. Willie Herenton, who later became the city's first Black mayor. When I inquired to confirm if the principal had received my letter, he told me that he had and would read it later. He placed the letter in his briefcase and left his office that day without reading it or responding to me. Neither the principal nor Superintendent responded to my letter.

I eventually heard from the principal by way of a letter. In his correspondence, I was informed that I had been declared "surplus" and would not return to Booker T. Washington as a coach. I contacted the principal and inquired why such action was being taken. He told me that the men did not want me coaching football and he had to keep the other coaches happy. It was clear that this was sexual discrimination.

I continued my retaliation by consulting and ultimately hiring a lawyer. Attorney Mark Allen was hired at a cost of $1,000.00 to defend me and get me reinstated to my coaching position. It only took two minutes to get justice to prevail for the moment. The attorney made a phone call to the superintendent of schools. The superintendent made a call to the principal and I was immediately reinstated. This kind of foolish behavior seesawed back and forth for three years. At the end of each of the next two years, I was notified that I would not be rehired as a coach for the next year. I went through the same procedure, I called the lawyer, the lawyer called the superintendent of schools, the superintendent called the principal who agreed to rehire me, the superintendent called the lawyer, who called me to say I had my job back. It was a case of justice prevailing each time. I got tired of all this, however. But, I was determined to keep up the fight.

The opposition kept on coming. In the year of 1988, Memphis deregulated some of its schools. This meant that teachers in those schools were required to reapply for the position they wanted, even if it were the same position held the previous year. Teachers had to go before a committee appointed by the Board of Education. The committee consisted of teachers from other schools, assistant principals, and principals, as well as parents. When you went before the committee, you were asked questions pertaining to your teaching philosophy and how you would deal with students in certain situations.

I thought I passed my examination, but I was not chosen to return to Booker T. Washington. I learned later that all the parents were favorable of me. When parents came to me later on, they told me of the origin of the problem. They said in unison, "The principal said to the committee that you would not return to Booker T. Washington no matter what they said or did." The parents kept me informed because they wanted me back at Booker T. Washington. They felt I was a good teacher as well as a good coach. But, the parents did more than that, they went to the superintendent of schools and protested the principal's actions. Eventually, I was reassigned to the school.

I had the hard decision of whether I should go back to Booker T. Washington. Teachers called me teary-eyed and weeping over the phone and told me that the principal had put it out that he was going to "get my job". I loved Booker T. Washington, but I did not want to jeopardize my job. I was in a dilemma. The frustrations and stress became overwhelming. I decided not to return to Booker T. Washington High School.

I talked to the principal at Geeter Junior High School, Mr. Joe Emmons, about my predicament and inquired of some opening there. In 1989, I was accepted at Geeter Junior High School as a teacher of science, health, and physical education as well as coach of the girls track team. Arriving at Geeter in the Fall of 1989, I went straight to work. Without pay, I assisted as coach of the football team. For two years in a row, we came close to winning the championship. In addition, the recognitions kept on coming. For the school years of 1988 and 1989,

I was named among the **Who's Who in American Education.**

A feeling of disgust and humiliation, however, continued to gnaw at me. It did not allow me to entertain a feeling of comfort. Restlessness consumed me. I was not at ease until I made the decision to pursue justice at a higher level. I knew I had been discriminated against because of my sex. I could not rest until I obtained some inner sense of satisfaction.

On August 6, 1990, I requested an appearance before the school board of the Memphis City Schools. My request was granted. When I stood before the officials of Memphis' educational system, I made the following statement.

TO: Superintendent Herenton, Board President, Board
        Members, Concerned Parents, Teachers and Students

My name is Coach Shirley McCray - Teacher/Coach and History Maker. I have 23 dedicated years with the Memphis City School System - 15 years as the first woman Football Coach in the city, state and nation.

I am here to inform you of the unfair treatment, sexual discrimination and character assassination of me as a coach by Mr. Patterson. It would take at least 3 days, not 3 minutes to tell it all. However, I will try and keep it short. If any members of the Board would like further proof, I'll be glad to talk with you.

I came to Booker T. Washington in 1986 as an assistant football coach (head junior varsity) at the request of Mr. Patterson. I also coached and assisted in girls' track and girls' basketball. I was cheerleader sponsor, senior sponsor and program director over all programs in the school - and - community service worker. My duties mentioned above should let you know that I love my school, students and the community, and I didn't mind working 12 to 15 hours a day helping some boy or girl to be successful in life.

It seemed that the other football coaches at Booker T. Washington did not want a woman coaching football. I was told that the football field was no place for a woman. They were very vulgar and abusive towards me.

138

I was cursed and berated in the presence of the football players. On one occasion, I was told by one of the coaches that I should take my *blank, blank, blank* inside and wash the clothes and clean-up the locker room and be glad to get paid for that. I was reassigned by the head coach to wash uniforms and clean-up the locker room that year. The men coaches didn't do that - only me. On another occasion - game situation - a player came to me to ask directions. I was just about to give directions when this coach came up and grabbed the boy in the chest, pushed him away from me and said, "Don't ask her a blank thing! She can't coach! Ask me M - F!" There were several occasions on which these kinds of things occurred.

A letter (documented with times and dates) was given to Mr. Patterson, a copy sent to Dr. Herenton and the area supervisor informing them of the discrimination and abusiveness of the coaches, and a conference requested. Mr. Patterson put the letter in his briefcase and said he would read it later and left the office. Mr. Patterson never had a conference with the football coaching staff to discuss and attempt to resolve the problems that existed.

After the season was over, I was informed by Mr. Patterson that I would not be coaching football - REASON - the men didn't want me coaching football and he had to keep the other coaches happy. Apparently, Mr. Patterson agreed with them. No other reason was given. Mr. Patterson never observed me as a coach because he didn't attend games that my junior varsity team played. He never observed me during football practice. His decision to fire me as a coach certainly was not based on my coaching ability. Might I add here, that my team was second in the division. It won more games than the senior teams put together. It seems like just plain sexual discrimination.

Because of what I felt to be sexual discrimination, I went to a legal advisor, who, in turn, had a conference with Dr. Herenton. I was re-assigned to the football coaching position. The following two years the same thing happened - I was fired as football coach. In 1987

I was also declared surplus. (It seems that Mr. Patterson was attempting to get rid of me in any way that he could.) I again went to my legal advisor and was re-assigned to Booker T. Washington as a football coach.

When Booker T. Washington became a deregulated school, I was not reassigned there. I was interviewed - everyone on the school committee was in favor of me being assigned to Booker T. Washington except Mr. Patterson. I was informed by a group of parents that Mr. Patterson told them he was not going to allow me to return to Booker T. Washington no matter what they said or did. Parents in the community protested to Dr. Herenton, and I was eventually reassigned to Booker T. Washington.

I was told by friends who worked at Booker T. Washington that Mr. Patterson was spreading the word that he was going to make it as hard as he could for me and try to get my job. Many of my students and parents were very upset and angered by the whole situation. I had gone through enough frustration, agony and stress with Mr. Patterson, fighting to keep my position as a football coach at Booker T. Washington. Also, I did not want my students to be caught in the middle. Therefore, I decided not to return to Booker T. Washington in 1989.

In spite of it all, however, I still want to coach - any sport. I'm a coach and I love coaching but I cannot get a coaching position. It seems that Mr. Patterson has put out the word among principals not to hire me as a coach.

It seems very strange that although I've been recognized nationally as a winning football coach - I have a total of 23 years coaching and teaching experience. I am a winning coach and a very good instructor - my record speaks for itself. I work diligently with my students and parents in the community. Yet, I cannot get a coaching position in the Memphis City Schools. I have been discriminated against, lied on, misused and black-balled from coaching because of Mr. Patterson.

Something is very wrong, ladies and gentlemen. I would like to encourage you as a Board to investigate this situation. Please don't let my coaching be in vain.

Thank you,
Coach Shirley McCray

August 6, 1990

My meeting with the school board was successful in that as of that meeting, the principal of Booker T. Washington, Mr. Dorsey Patterson, was removed and assigned to a position at the city schools Pupil Services Center. In the process of repositioning Mr. Patterson, he came under investigation for possibly altering students school attendance records. He later was adjudged in error for altering records and was threatened with reduction in salary as punitive action.

I proceeded with a vengeance to assault the Board of Education to restore my integrity and feeling of decency. I felt I had been wronged and I wanted to be vindicated. It was like a football game I was playing. It was like the time I played sandlot football and got hit so hard that my lights went out. When I took the ball that day, I ran with it as hard as I could because I was trying to make a touchdown. Least of my concerns was getting tackled, let alone the physical injury that might occur. Similarly, I took the ball in this case and ran so hard with it that if I had gotten hit and my lights had gone out, it did not matter. I was not going to lose this contest by default. I was going to show up on the field and run the ball no matter what the outcome, regardless of whether I was knocked out. I decided that the hurt, the injury, the pain, could not be more than I already had endured. I had to live with myself. I had to fight back.

On August 27, 1990, I sent the following letter to the Atlanta Regional office of the U. S. Department of Education's Office of Civil Rights.

August 27, 1990

Mr. Thomas A. Stevens
Regional Director
Atlanta Region
U. S. Department of Education
Office of Civil Rights
P. O. Box 1777, Suite 2221
Atlanta, Georgia 30301-043060

Dear Mr. Stevens:

The enclosed is being sent to your attention and
constitutes a formal complaint to the U. S. Department
of Education, Office of Civil Rights. I am charging
the Memphis Board of Education, through its
superintendent of schools and the principal and coaching
staff at Booker T. Washington High School with sexual
discrimination and harassment. I have been denied the
opportunity to coach football, despite my demonstrated
competency in this area, because I am female.

Please feel free to contact me if you need additional
information regarding the case presented. Thank you
for your attention to this matter.

> Very Truly yours,
> Shirley Yvonne McCray
> 3774 Claree Drive
> Memphis, Tn. 38116
> (901) 345-0940

I continued relentlessly in filing complaints, everywhere I could.
I filed a complaint with the TENNESSEE HUMAN RIGHTS COMMIS-
SION. I received responses almost immediately. On September 11,
1990, I received a letter from the Atlanta office of the EEOC stating they
had begun to investigate my claim. Nine months later, I received a letter from Timothy Williams, an investigator with EEOC notifying me
that my case had been assigned to him. Within a period of one year
and one month following my receipt of that letter, the whole matter
was resolved.

Throughout the ensuing year, deliberations and negotiations were
carried on. Bargains were offered to me. Some of them began to look

rather appealing. Finally, we struck upon an arrangement which was satisfactory. The settlement was three-fold: 1) I was to receive back pay for the time I was out of a job coaching football, and 2) a position was opened at Geeter Junior High School as a paid assistant coach in football. I would remain at this position until 3) Booker T. Washington was renovated. Once Booker T. Washington was renovated, I would return there under the same conditions I had before I left that school. As a matter of compromise, I was asked to agree in a formally signed statement that I had never been discriminated against. Of course, everyone in Memphis knew different.

To climax the entire episode, I received a letter from Nashville, Tennessee stating officially that I had not been discriminated against.

October 27, 1992

Ms. Shirley Y. H. McCray
3774 Claree Drive
Memphis, TN 38207

RE: McCray vs Memphis Board of Education
        Charge #: 250-87-0971

Dear Ms. McCray:

Under the authority vested in me by EEOC's regulations, I issue on behalf of the Commission, the following determination as to the merits of the subject charge.

Respondent is an employer within the meaning of Title VII and timeliness, deferral, and all other jurisdictional requirements have been met.

Based on certified acceptance of the findings of the Tennessee Human Rights Commission, I concluded that there is not reasonable cause to believe that the charge is true.

This determination concludes EEOC's processing of the subject charge. As the charge alleged a Title VII violation, this is notice that if the Charging Party wishes to pursue this matter further, she may do so by filing a private action in U.S. District Court against the Respondent(s) named above within 90 days of receipt of this Determination. Once this 90 day period is over, the right to sue will be lost.

On Behalf of the Commission,

_____   10-28-92
W. S. Grabon, District Director   Date

The conclusion of the matter left something to be desired, although I got what I wanted in terms of placement and an opportunity to coach — with pay. The officials did not openly admit culpability in the case, although unofficially and privately they acknowledged that wrongdoing had taken place. It seemed that institutionally, sex discrimination was a thing to be grasped.

But, I knew I had been vindicated, God was my witness. I had the feeling of Job of the Bible, when his false accusers came to him with their menacing remarks. His response was,

> . . . behold, my witness is in heaven,
> and my record is on high.
> Job 16:19

In the Fall of 1992, I returned to Booker T. Washington under a different principal and a different coach. I strove to build a winning junior varsity program. In 1995, my team came close to winning the district championship. We lost by only four points, 20-16. I was proud of my team, just as I have been over the years.

Coach McCray shows how it's done on the field at Booker T. Washington

Situations should change, but they never do — only the people and places. Even now, in spite of all the evidence, some people say I am not the first woman to coach an all male football team. Others say I am. The facts stated in this story stand; and more than that, God is my witness. Just as importantly, I

144

Coach McCray leads the way for her Warriors at Booker T. Washington

lasted and held out more than anyone. I spent 24 years in the sunshine and the rain, in the sleet and snow, in hot weather and cold, in good times and bad. I endured it all. But the prize of them all is the 1,500 young boys I coached, whose lives I touched and molded for good.

Now that I am retiring, I do so hoping that my aggressiveness and determination will open a door for another young lady. Maybe what I did in the 60's at Memphis State University and in my career as the first woman to coach an all male football team, will do for some modern-day young woman coming behind me what Dr. Martin Luther King, Jr., did for the Black and poor of this world.

*Coach McCray and her last football team —
Booker T. Washington Warriors, 1996-97.*

THE BRIDGE BUILDER

An old man, going a lone highway,
Came at the evening, cold and gray,
To a chasm, vast and deep and wide,
Through which was flowing a sullen tide.
The old man crossed in the twilight dim;
The sullen stream had no fears for him;
But he turned when safe on the other side
And built a bridge to span the tide.

"Old man," said a fellow pilgrim near,
"You are wasting strength with building here;
Your journey will end with the ending day;
You never again must pass this way;
You have crossed the chasm, deep and wide —
Why build you the bridge at the eventide?"

The builder lifted his old gray head:
"Good friend, in the path I have come," he said,
"There followeth after me today
A youth whose feet must pass this way.
This chasm that has been naught to me
To that fair-haired youth may a pitfall be.
He, too, must cross in the twilight dim;
Good friend, I am building the bridge for him"

Will Allen Dromgoole, ? - d. 1934

CHAPTER XVIII

LIVES I HAVE TOUCHED: THE LIVING LEGACY I LEAVE BEHIND

If I can help somebody, as I pass along,
If I can cheer somebody, with a word or a song,
If I can show somebody, he is going wrong,
Then my living, shall not be in vain.

If I can do my duty, as a Christian ought,
If I can bring back beauty, to a world upwrought,
If I can spread Love's message, as The Master taught
Then my living, shall not be in vain.

Then, my living shall not be in vain,
Then, my living shall not be in vain,
If I can help somebody, as I pass along,
Then my living shall not be in vain.

Living out of my grandmother's philosophy, I learned that the best I could ever do was to "help people." I learn that I could "be somebody" by helping others to "be somebody." That is what I have spent my career as a coach trying to do.

I have sought to bequeath to the world, young people I tried to develop into "somebodies" so as they assumed life's responsibilities, they could make the world a better place. The persons cited below are only some of those whose lives I touched as I passed along this way as teacher, coach, counselor, mentor, doctor, lawyer, surrogate mother, big sister, and friend.

Larry Finch (2nd from R). I taught him at Melrose High School. He went on to become head basketball coach at Memphis State University.

Top:
Toni Williams. Ran track and played basketball at Booker T. Washington. Currently, she teaches at Fairley and coaches volleyball and softball for girls.

Middle:
Toni Williams (L) and Tarus Wilkins (R). Tarus Wilkins is a teacher in daycare in Memphis.

Bottom:
Nathan Cole. I coached him at Chickasaw Junior High School. He is head track coach at Westwood High School.

Linda F. Lanton
Riverview Junior High School
Lawyer, architectural engineer,
Motorola Executive

Rufus Gunn
Chickasaw Junior High School
Supervisor at Memphis Light,
Gas, & Water

Eric Wrushen
Chickasaw Junior High School
Electrical engineer
Houston, Texas

Anthony Holland
Geeter Junior High School
Student at University of Memphis

Steve Becton
Chickasaw Junior High School
Coach and teacher
White Station High School

Kila Jones
Booker T. Washington
Receptionist

Candis Golden
Booker T. Washington
Receptionist

Iris Wilson
Booker T. Washington
Social Security Office,
U. S. Government

T. Pettis
Booker T. Washington
Radiologist at Memphis Hospital

Yolanda Williams
Booker T. Washington
House wife and mother

Jean Killerbrew
Riverview Junior High School
She is a hospital attendant
in Memphis.

Vincent Aldridge
Chickasaw Junior High School
Lawyer
Houston, Texas

Cheyenne Gibson
Chickasaw Junior High School &
Westwood Community Center
Professional basketball player

Darian Sharp
Chickasaw Junior High School
Senior Analyst
Federal Express Corporation

Baskerville Holmes
Chickasaw Junior High School
Professional Basketball Player
(Deceased)

Reverend Michael Dear
Chickasaw Junior High School
Minister

Reverend Terrance Trent
Chickasaw Junior High School
Minister

These are not all, there are so many, many more!!!

FORMULA FOR BEING SUCCESSFUL IN COACHING
(The following philosophy carried me for 30 years)

1. Be a Spiritual person
   Believe in a Superior Being
   Be active in a church
   Take your team to church with you.

2. Be honest, trustworthy, respectful, and loyal
   to players and other coaches.

3. Show a great deal of initiative and ambition.

4. Be a good mixer. Get along with players, community,
   and other coaches. Take time to talk with players
   and listen to their problems.

5. Think of your players as human beings, not a commodity.

6. Set good examples. Be good role models.

7. Inspire your athletes to a degree they think and
   know they are capable of doing what it takes to win.

8. Don't be afraid to show love.

9. Refrain from using abusive words about or to your players.

10. Stay positive.

"It's All In A State Of Mind"

If you think you are beaten, you are;
If you think you dare not, you won't;
If you like to win, but don't think you can,
It's almost a cinch you won't.

If you think you'll lose, you're lost;
For out in the world you'll find
Success begins with a fellow's will'
It's all in a state of mind.

For many a game is lost
Ere even a play is run,
And many a coward fails
ere even his work is begun.

Think big and your deeds will grow,
Think small and you'll fall behind;
think that you CAN and you WILL;
It's all in a state of mind.

If you think you are out-classed, you are;
You've got to think high to rise;
You've got to be sure of yourself before
You can ever win a prize.

Life's battles don't always go
To the stronger or faster man,
But sooner or later, the man who wins
Is the fellow who thinks he can.

> *Walter D. Wintle*
> *Quoted from*
> *Bear Bryant On Winning Football*
> *Paul "Bear" Bryant*
> *Prentice-Hall, Inc.*